Shake the Money Tree

How to Produce a Winning Fundraising Event with a Live and Silent Auction

Richard O'Keef

Richard O'Keef Fund-Raising Auctions
Salt Lake City, Utah
www.letsdoanauction.com

For contact information please refer to:
www.letsdoanauction.com/contact.htm

Library of Congress Cataloging-in-Publication Data
O'Keef, Richard
Shake the Money Tree: How to Produce a Winning Fundraising Event with a Live and Silent Auction / Richard O'Keef
ISBN 0-9787884-1-9
1. Event planning. 2. Benefit auctions. I. Title.

Disclaimer
This book is as a guide only, and does not claim to be the final definitive word on any of the subjects covered. The statements made and opinions expressed are the personal observations and assessments of the author based on his own experiences and are not intended to prejudice any party. There may be errors and omissions in this guide. As such, the author does not accept any liability or responsibility for any loss or damage that may have been caused, or alleged to have been caused, through use of the information contained in this manual. Errors or omissions will be corrected in future editions, provided the author receives written notification of such.

Acknowledgments

Thanks to all the auction chairs, executive directors, development directors, board members, volunteers, Auctioneers, audio/video engineers, caterers, celebrities, entertainers, journalists, florists, DJs, special event providers, emcees, donors, and guests that have contributed, whether knowingly or not, to the creation of this book.

Special thanks goes to: Jan Hopkins, Freelance writer; Judy Magid, Arts, Entertainment and Culture Reporter for the Salt Lake Tribune; Kim Henage, Director of Events, Boys and Girls Clubs of South Valley, Utah; Sarah Noel, Special Events Manager, Juvenile Diabetes Research Foundation Indiana State Chapter; Roni Thomas, Communications Manager, Salt Lake Art Center; Pam Boede, Development Officer, Salt Lake Community Action Program – Head Start; Debi Gilmore, Member of West Ridge Academy Board of Directors, President of West Ridge Academy Advisory Council; Lisa Burbidge, Development Director, Ronald McDonald House Charities of the Intermountain Area; Dick & Sharon Friel, Charity Auctioneers, Seattle Washington; and Carolyn Abaunza, writer.

About the Author

Richard O'Keef has helped non-profit organizations plan and carry out hundreds of successful fundraisers. As an Auctioneer he is a master at entertaining audiences while getting top dollar for auction items. He says the mark of a good Auctioneer is when he can get a lot of money from his audience, and then they thank HIM on their way out.

Richard is a 1992 graduate of the Missouri Auction School, and has gone on to become a leading fundraising Auctioneer. In his spare time he jogs and runs marathons. He says jogging helps him sustain his enthusiasm during the longer auctions. He learned Japanese to conduct an auction for a predominantly Japanese audience. He also holds an MBA degree.

Richard has developed what he calls the "The Four Objectives of a Successful Fundraiser", which he supports with dozens of proven strategies and shares in detail with the organizations he serves. His ability to entertain and make people feel good about donating to a cause, are traits for which Richard has become well known. He is founder of Richard O'Keef Fund-Raising Auctions based out of Salt Lake City, Utah.

Introduction

I've written this book to help fundraising organizers everywhere raise more money to help more people. I know that a lot of work goes into planning and executing a successful fundraiser, so I've tried to make this book easy to read, practical, and to the point.

The main portion of the book is comprised of tasks. All tasks are organized within committees. Each committee is headed by a chairperson for whom I write. I understand that not all committees are built the same. But I have determined that the best way to find specific information in this book is to look it up by committee and task.

Each task is assigned a number that will be used as a reference throughout the entire book. By arranging the book like this, tasks can refer to other tasks by their task numbers. For instance, reference to the sound system is made in multiple places, but explained in detail in only one place: Sound System (10.25).

When you are referred to a task number, you can flip to that task number if you want to know more detail regarding that task – and then return to where you were reading. You can look at the table of contents for a list of all the tasks and their numbers. The table of contents is a lot like a things-to-do-list so you won't let important tasks go unattended.

Some tasks may not apply to your particular fundraising event. For example, your small, quaint fundraiser may not have all the glamour and glitz of a large fancy gala. If that is the case, simply skim over the tasks involving glamour and glitz and focus only on what pertains to your event.

I've tried to include tasks that can be used for all types of fundraising events. If a certain task is not in your immediate future, just skip over it. But I suspect if you continue to be involved in planning fundraisers, you *will* have an interest in all these tasks at one time or another.

There are places in this book where I refer to various websites. But because websites can become obsolete, I don't list them here. Instead, I list them on my own website in order to keep them up to date. To visit those links, go to:

www.LetsDoAnAuction.com/resources.htm

Have fun with this book, and may your next fundraiser be the most successful ever.

Richard O'Keef

Table of Contents

Shake the Money Tree

The Four Objectives of a Successful Fundraiser

I make sure my microphone is on, my shirt is tucked in, and my zipper is up as I stand off stage waiting for my introduction. My adrenaline is starting to pump. I take a deep breath and exhale.

"And now let me introduce our Auctioneer," says the emcee. I take another deep breath. This time I hold it in. "Please welcome, Richard O'Keef".

Polite applause.

I begin walking quickly toward the stage. As I do so, I begin bid-calling into my microphone, slowly at first, but rhythmically.

> "Five dollar now ten now fifteen dollar now a twenty now five twenty five and now thirty now five thirty five and now…"

I pause for a short moment. I'm at center stage now. Some of the talkative crowd has now turned their attention toward me, but most are still visiting with each other. I shift into high speed, show-off mode, intent on getting everyone's attention.

> "40 bid-it-at 40 would you give 40 40 to buy 'em would you give 40 able to buy 'em would you bid 40 now 5 45 bid-it-at 45 now 50 dollar now 50 where would you give 50 now 55 55 bid-it-at 55 now 60…"

My lips are popping out the numbers as I go through the 60's, the 70's, 80's, 90's, and end with, "…and now a hundred dollar bill." Without a pause I reach my arm out to the audience and say,

> "Ladies and gentlemen, welcome to the live auction portion of our program tonight. I'm Richard O'Keef, and I'll be your Auctioneer."

Air rushes into my lungs as I gasp for a breath. The audience applauds and I am off again, doing that for which I have developed a passion: conducting a fundraising auction.

I've been an Auctioneer since 1992 when I graduated from the Missouri Auction School. After that short 15-day course, I helped an Auctioneer with a household estate auction, another with a business liquidation auction, and then I did my first charity auction – and the first auction by myself. It was a Boy Scout cake sale. It was the first time they had used a "Professional Auctioneer" and even though I was still pretty green, I helped them raise more money than ever before. What a great feeling. I had found my niche.

Not long after my debut as a fundraising Auctioneer, I came to discover that not all fundraising auctions were created equally. Some auctions were very successful; that is, they raised a lot of money and guests seem to have a good time.

Other auctions did not fare so well, failing to raise enough money to make up for the labor and expense that went into them, and leaving committee members frustrated and disappointed, vowing never to be in charge of a fundraiser again. What was the difference? If I was to become an effective fundraising Auctioneer, I had to find out. I wanted a formula for success; one that would result in a successful fundraising auction every time it was followed.

Over the next several years I started paying close attention to what made successful fundraisers successful and what made the others less than successful. In order to measure the success of a fundraiser, I had to define just what a successful fundraiser was. I wanted to keep it simple and measurable. Here is what I came up with:

A successful fundraising auction is when guests give you a lot of their money, and then thank YOU on their way home.

I liked it but it was not very measurable. "A lot of money" meant that financial goals were met or exceeded. The "thanks" from your guests indicated they had a good time and looked forward to attending the next fundraiser.

I've actually seen guests thank the organizers for making it fun to spend money at their event. After one of my auctions, an attorney said to me, "That was the most eloquent, dignified and legal picking the pockets of the people I have ever seen." I would consider that to mean he had a good time, wouldn't you?

So, here is the revised version of the definition of a successful fundraiser. It is not as fun to say, but meets the "measurable" criteria better:

A successful fundraising auction is when we meet or exceed our financial goal and guests tell us they had a good time on their way home.

Since successful fundraisers require guests to be willing, and even anxious to part with their money, I looked for things that gave people reasons to feel generous. I also looked for things that caused people to feel tightfisted with their money. I made an interesting discovery. I discovered there are things (or tasks) that you, your committee, your volunteers and your Auctioneer can do that will make people feel good about spending money.

There are also things, I discovered, that you, your committee, your volunteers and your Auctioneer can do, or fail to do, that will take away the desire or inhibit or discourage people from spending money. We want to eliminate those things, and take away all the excuses that cause people to feel un-generous.

You see, generosity is an emotion, and the amount of money people spend at your fundraising event will depend on how they feel. From the moment your guests step into your event until the time they leave, they are in your realm of influence. What you do (or fail to do) during that time can make a difference in how generous your guests feel. Everything you do at your fundraiser should be to inspire generosity and remove any excuses that would discourage people from being generous.

> From the moment your guests step into your event until the time they leave, they are in your realm of influence. What you do (or fail to do) during that time can make a difference in how generous your guests feel.

The tasks presented in this book are designed to make your guests feel four different emotions while attending your event. I've discovered that the more you do to cause these emotions to surface within your guests, the more generous your guests will feel, and the more money you'll raise. By becoming aware of these emotions, you will understand the reasons for which I present the tasks. Here are the four emotions that will cause your guests to feel generous at your fundraiser. Refer back to them periodically. This is the rationale behind the advice and tasks taught in this book. This is what's going to make your fundraiser successful:

If your guests (1) feel like royalty, (2) get choked up with emotion over your cause, (3) want what you're selling, and (4) discover the thrill of bidding, not only will

they give you a lot of their money, they will thank YOU on their way out.

The purpose of the tasks suggested in this book is to empower you to awaken these four emotions within your guests while they are at your event. Here is another way to put it. I call this **"The Four Objectives of a Successful Fundraiser"**. You want to make your guests:

1. Feel important
2. Gain a desire to support your cause
3. Want what you're selling
4. Get caught up in the thrill of bidding

I will refer to these four objectives throughout this book. These objectives apply to the whole event, not just to the live and silent auction pieces of the event. When you, your committee, your volunteers and your Auctioneer focus on achieving these four objectives, your fundraiser will have the best chance of being the most successful ever.

When I stand in front of an audience as an Auctioneer, charged with the responsibility of raising a lot of money, if the first three of the **Four Objectives of a Successful Fundraiser** have been met, my job is easy. All I have to do is get the audience to feel the thrill of bidding. When all four objectives are met, guess what happens? Guests feel generous and we raise a lot of money.

Now that we know WHAT makes people feel generous, we need to answer the question: HOW do we achieve those objectives? Here is the answer simply stated:

1. Guests can be made to feel important by <u>pampering</u> and <u>entertaining</u> them.
2. Guests can gain a desire to support your cause by <u>educating</u> them and making an <u>emotional appeal</u>.
3. Guests can develop a desire to want what you're selling by applying pro9ven <u>marketing techniques</u>.

4. Guests can get caught up in the thrill of bidding by putting <u>show-business</u> into the live auction.

The following page is a summary of what I've explained, and the foundation for the rest of the book.

Primary Goals:
1. Meet or exceed our financial goal
2. Have guests thank us on their way home

Objective 1:
Guests must be made to feel important.

> **How:** Pamper them
> Entertain them

Objective 2:
Guests must gain a desire to support our cause.

> **How:** Educate them
> Make an emotional appeal

Objective 3:
Guests must want to buy what we're selling.

> **How:** Use proven marketing techniques

Objective 4:
Guests must get caught up in the thrill of bidding.

> **How:** Put show-business into the live
> auction

Goal #1

The first primary goal is to "Meet or exceed our financial goal". This book discusses many different ideas and strategies to raise money. They include establishing a financial goal and creating a budget; procuring items to sell; finding in-kind services, sponsors and underwriters; finding and keeping volunteers; inviting guests and giving guests multiple opportunities to contribute.

Goal #2

The second primary goal is to "Have guests thank us on their way home". This is an indication that they've had fun. If **The Four Objectives of a Successful Fundraiser** were met, this goal will have been achieved and guests will look forward to attending your next annual fundraiser.

Pamper them

Guests are made to feel important with pampering. Tasks meant to pamper your guests are given in detail throughout this book. Have you ever talked to someone who has been on a cruise? What one thing were they most impressed with? Wasn't it how well they were pampered? They were pampered with food, entertainment, personal attention by the ship's staff, room service, and fun activities. You want your guests to come away from your event with the same feeling. So you will pamper them with things like valet parking, coat check, short waiting lines, gifts, surprises, personal attention, and great food. This book contains a plethora of ideas.

Entertain them

Guests are made to feel important with entertainment, which is also given a lot of attention throughout this book. The social hour and silent auction should be entertaining. The dinner should be entertaining. The live auction should be entertaining. Remember, you are in show-business. People are starved for entertainment. And as you satisfy that need, your guests will loosen their purse string. So we will cater to their short attention span by showering them with entertainment like photo opportunities, prize drawings, celebrity appearances, music, dance, compelling speakers and a glitzy live auction.

Educate Them

Guests will have a greater desire to support your cause if they learn about your cause. So you need to communicate to your guests just what it is you do; how you enhance lives; how you save lives; how you make a difference. We'll get into newsletters, newspaper articles, displays, pictures, posters, and notes.

Make an Emotional Appeal

Guests will have even a greater desire to support your cause if you stir their emotions. You do that by communicating to them why you do what you do. This is done with the emotional appeal. You are going to learn all about giving an emotional appeal; who should give it, how long it should be, and how to make it most effective. An emotional appeal can take the form of a speech, a PowerPoint presentation or a short video. We don't ask for tears, just misty eyes.

Use Proven Marketing Techniques

You want your guests to want to buy what you sell at your silent and live auctions. Smart marketing comes into play here. You will learn how to hold a pre-auction open house to market you big-ticket items, how to display auction items to draw attention, and in what order is best to sell items at the live auction.

Put Show-Business into the Live Auction

Guests will bid more often if they get caught up in the thrill of bidding. I love it when I hear a guest say, "That live auction was fun." And I love it when I hear Event Chairpersons say, "Wow. We raised more money tonight than we ever have." That happens when guests get caught up in the thrill of bidding. And guests get caught up in the thrill of bidding when show-business is thrown into your live auction. You will soon be a show-biz expert involved in the sound system, lighting, decorations, volunteers to be used during the live auction, and choosing the right Auctioneer.

Spy on Some Fundraisers

After you read this book, have some fun by conducting an experiment. Go visit some fundraisers put on by other organizations. Observe what they do to pamper and entertain their guests. See how their guests gain a desire (or fail to gain a desire) to support their cause. Notice how they market the items for sale, and how they put show-business into their live auction, and see if you don't agree with me, that the better an organization achieves **The Four Objectives of a Successful Fundraiser**, the more successful their fundraiser.

Establish a Steering Committee

It's a good idea to have access to people who can answer important questions, keep you out of legal trouble, give you marketing advice, and help you with finances. These people will be your Steering Committee. They don't have to come to all your meetings, just be there for you when you need them. They will understand, of course, that since you are a non-profit organization, their advice is given with no expectation of receiving payment other than the good feeling of knowing that they are helping to improve lives by helping you raise money.

You form a steering committee by asking people to help. There are many professionals who would feel good about being associated with a non-profit organization that does good things. In most cases, all you have to do is ask. A steering committee can be made up of people such as:

- Board members
- Legal council
- Financial advisors
- People who have done this before
- Sales and marketing experts
- Graphic designers

Description of Tasks by Committee

1. Event Chair

1.1 Catch the vision

Whether you are a staff member such as an Executive Director or Development Officer, or a brave volunteer Event Chair, you are about to embark on a mission to change people's lives; first your life, then your committees', then your guests', then the people for whom you will ultimately be raising money. That's a lot of lives to change. You have an awesome responsibility.

The organization that you are helping was started by someone who saw a need; who wanted to make a difference and felt compelled to do something about it. As the event chairperson, you have been entrusted with the responsibility to further that cause. If you catch that same vision, and share the same passion that inspired the birth of that organization, you'll have more fun, be a better leader, and achieve a greater sense of satisfaction than you would otherwise.

That's not all. Your enthusiasm will be contagious. It will spread to your committee chairpersons, and to your volunteers. Then, as your committee chairs and volunteers feel the fire that comes from you, they will be motivated. They will spread that spirit to potential donors when they ask for donations. You will procure more donations that will be bigger and better.

It doesn't stop there. As your influence spreads, the guests who attend your event will feel everyone's passion, which will cause your guests to have a greater desire to support your cause. When that happens, you will ultimately raise more money to change more lives of those destined to benefit from the fruits of your event. When you see how effectively your passion can pass from one to another, you will realize that your job is not about simply raising funds, but about building relationships. The relationships you build will last past your event, and perhaps out of those you mentor and motivate, some will take the reigns of event chairperson someday.

> Your job is not about simply raising funds, but about building relationships.

You will also form relationships with item donors and guests that visit your fundraiser. They too need to catch your enthusiasm and vision to continue the relationship with your organization, and carry on supporting its cause. The money you raise is a manifestation of the relationships you make and the bonds you create.

Good event chairpersons, volunteers and Auctioneers realize that what they are offering to the community is a chance to see a need, get involved, and make a difference. If that is the foundation of your fundraising efforts, applying the tasks and strategies in this book will seem natural and you will raise a lot of money.

It all starts with you. It all starts with catching the vision. Consider the following ways to do that:

1. Learn the organization's mission statement inside and out.
2. Learn all the services and programs the organization provides.
3. Learn where the money you raise will go.
4. Develop a relationship with board members.

5. Talk to staff members who provide the benefits of the organization.
6. Talk to people who have benefited from the organization.
7. Volunteer to help do what the organization does. Serve the people it serves. When you see the needs being satisfied first hand, you'll catch your vision.

Think Beyond Your Event

Because you are in the business of building relationships, it's natural to think beyond your event. If you cannot get people to help with your event this year, ask them if they would be interested in helping next year – even if you're not going to be the Event Chair next year. Most Event Chairs are so preoccupied with their event, they forget to look ahead. Here are some examples of looking ahead.

- You ask someone to donate a fabulous auction item and they tell you it's not budgeted. So you ask, "Will you give it to us next year for next year's fundraiser?"
- You procure an item. As you walk out the door, you turn around and say, "By the way, would you give this to us again next year?"
- You ask someone who would make a wonderful emcee to help with your upcoming event but they've already made plans. "Well, how about next year? We would love to have you work with us at next year's fundraiser."
- You ask a celebrity to attend your event and they decline because of a prior commitment. Hit them up for next year. "Do you suppose you could make it to next year's event?"
- You ask a company to buy a table at your event and they have run out of budget money. "We'd love to have you come to next year's event. Do you think we could make it into next year's budget?

- You invite a wealthy philanthropist to be a guest at your event and he or she cannot make it. "Well, let's stay in touch. We'd love it if you could make it to next year's event."
- You ask the editor of a local magazine to do a feature article about your organization and they say they are pretty full for this year. So you can say, "Well that's all right, we'll provide you with information so maybe next year you'll write a feature article on us." Then make sure someone stay's in touch.
- Your event is over. The money is in. The guests have gone home. Now you ensure that everyone who contributed gets thanked (14.1).

Think Beyond the Money

If you are thinking about doing your fundraiser only for the money, then you will miss out on some valuable opportunities:

- **Public awareness and exposure** – Your marketing, advertising and feature articles in newspapers and magazines can make people in the community aware of your organization, what it does, where the money goes, how it helps people, etc. etc. More public awareness can mean more successful fundraisers in the future.
- **Recruitment** – People with whom you come in contact (donors, volunteers, guests at your event) will get a chance to feel your enthusiasm and discover how fabulous your organization is. They may become long-time friends of your organization; perhaps become a staff member, a chairperson, a volunteer, or a major contributor. Consider every person you or your committee talks with to be a potential donor, resource, or volunteer; if not this year, maybe sometime in the future. There are people out there

looking to get involved in a charity. They surface during fundraising events. The next person you talk with might be one of them.

Two Burning Questions You Need to Answer

As an Event Chairperson, you need to establish (1) a financial goal and (2) a compelling reason why you are raising the money. You will be asked these two questions by potential donors and prospective guests:

1. How much are you trying to raise?
2. What is the money going to be used for?

If you, your committee chairs or your volunteers answer by saying, "Well, we're trying to raise as much as possible, and I think the money goes into some sort of general fund," you're going to feel unprepared and look unimpressive.

A better response would be: "We're planning to raise $175,000. The money is going to be used to expand our learning center with books and three new computers. We're going to provide more medical screening, immunizations and dental services to children who wouldn't get them otherwise. We're going to purchase better audio/visual equipment to educate the pubic. We're going to increase our staff to handle the increasing need for our services. We need to buy a new van to replace our old clunker so our people will be warm and safe.

The point is, you need to provide strong compelling reasons that committee chairs, volunteers, prospective donors and guests can visualize and get excited about. People will be more inclined to get involved if they know "how much" and "what for".

The second objective in the **Four Objectives of a Successful Fundraiser** is to help guests develop a greater desire to support your cause. We do this by educating and making an emotional appeal. You can start by sharing your financial goal and compelling reasons to raise money – with everyone. Use it in the Event Fact Sheet (1.12), your advertising, marketing, invitations, newsletters, feature articles and personal contacts. Get everyone routing, cheering and supporting you like you were the home team in the final playoff game.

> People will be more inclined to get involved if they know "how much" and "what for".

1.2   Establish the budget

Establishing the budget is one of the most exciting things you are going to do as an Event Chair. It is during this task that you forecast how much money you are going to make and how you are going to make it. Then, when you, your chairpersons and your volunteers go around telling people of your financial goal, you can all really believe it's obtainable and feel committed to it.

In fact, I'm going to be so bold as to suggest that you and your volunteers can expect to raise more money than the goal you set. I'm going to show you how to make that happen. With that thought in the back of everyone's mind, it will be easy to tell potential donors and prospective guests how much you are going to raise, because it will seem achievable.

Don't just go for the money. Think in terms of what the money will be used to purchase. What does your organization need the money for? Make a list. Imagine everything on that list becoming a reality – because that's what you are going to make happen. How good does that feel? Now put a price on it.

Let's say you need $120,000. Next, you need to put your sources of revenue and expenses on a spreadsheet and manipulate the numbers until your financial goal is realized on "paper". Consider the following simplified spreadsheet example.

Source of Revenue	**Goal**
Single ticket sales (500 guests at $100 per ticket)	$ 50,000
In-kind services (serves to decrease expenses)	
Underwriters	5,000
Cash contributions	5,000
Sponsors	10,000
Table purchases (10 tables at $1,300 per table)	13,000
Drawing (240 tickets at $5.00 per ticket)	1,200
Sale of centerpieces (30 out of 60 at $10 each)	300
Silent auction	20,000
Live auction	50,000
Fund-a-Program	20,000
Mini-store	1,000

Expected gross revenue	175,500

Expenses

Venue rental	$10,000
Advertising	5,000
Food and catering	20,000
Centerpieces	1,000
Party favors	1,000
Audio/visual	1,500
Lighting equipment	100
Entertainment and Auctioneer	2,500
Drinks	1,400
Valet services	1,000
Decorations	4,000
Printing	5,000
Postage	2,000
Photography	1,000

Expected expenses	55,500
Estimated Net Income	$120,000

In this example, we take all sources of revenue that we will be using, and come up with a total of $175,500. Then we list all the expenses we expect to incur and come up with a total of $55,500.

Revenue and expenses will be more realistic if we have records from last year's event. If you don't have a prior history of revenue and expenses, you're going to have to make an educated guess. Talk with other fundraising organizations that can help with estimating amounts.

When you subtract the estimated expenses from the expected gross revenue, you get an estimated net income. This example shows $120,000 – just what we need.

Estimate the Value of Auction Items
You Need to Procure

A large portion of your revenue will come from the live and silent auctions. When it comes to the live and silent auction items, it would be helpful to know what percent of retail value the items sold for at last year's event. For example, did the items sell for 50%, 60%, or maybe 70% of retail value?

If you are fortunate enough to have been given a Post-Event Evaluation (1.20) from last year's event, you can estimate the value of the live and silent auction items you need to procure to reach your live and silent auction goals this year. Let me illustrate.

In the sample spreadsheet above, the source of revenue from live and silent auctions total $70,000 (Silent auction: $20,000 plus live auction: $50,000). If last year, the live and silent auction items sold, on average, for 65% of retail value, and you feel like the same will happen again this year, then you will need to procure auction items worth $107,700 ($70,000/.65 rounded). In other words, you will need to gather, scrounge, solicit, and collect $107,700 worth of merchandise for the live and silent auctions to generate $70,000 in auction sales.

If data from last year's auctions are not available, a realistic assumption to make is that you will get 50% of retail value, on average, from your live and silent auctions. In other words, you'll need to come up with $140,000 worth of goods for your live and silent auctions to realize your goal of $70,000. ($70,000/.5 = $140,000).

If this analysis discourages you, don't worry. You're going to learn some great ways to procure items and services. You're also about to learn how to raise that percentage.

Expect to Exceed Your Financial Goal

I mentioned earlier that you should expect to exceed your financial goal. By working on achieving **The Four Objectives of a Successful Fundraiser**, you create an environment where your guests tend to feel more generous. Assuming that generosity will increase, and you have procured $140,000 worth of live and silent auction items from the example above, let's create another scenario:

- Instead of getting 50% of retail value from your live and silent auctions, you get 85% or $119,000. That's $49,000 more than the $70,000 originally predicted. Add $49,000 to estimated net income.
- You raise 50% more on Fund-a-Program than budget predicted. Add $10,000 to estimated net income.

In-kind services have been ignored so far. What if you were able to make the following happen as well?

- In-kind services resulted in a 25% reduction in expenses. Add $14,000 to estimated net income.

Estimated net income now becomes $193,000, or $73,000 greater than the originally forecasted amount of $120,000. In this example, you can expect to raise somewhere between $120,000 and $193,000. Once you share this information with your committees, the board, the staff and the volunteers, it is easy for them to believe that $120,000 is realistic and achievable. Then when your people solicit items and invite guests, and share your financial goal, they'll do it with conviction and confidence.

Please keep in mind that the previous example is for demonstration purposes only and amounts shown here should not be considered typical for any fundraising event.

Expenses

Consider grouping your expenses into three categories:

1. **Fixed expenses**. These expenses remain constant no matter how many guests attend. They would include postage, venue rental, marketing, printing, signage, audio-visual equipment, gasoline, entertainment fees, Auctioneer fee, sound system, stage and room decorations, security person, etc.
2. **Variable expenses**. These expenses depend on the number of people attending your event. They would include food, beverage, table and chair rental, center-piece cost, etc.
3. **Surprise expenses**. No matter how hard you try, there are always going to be surprise expenses; expenses nobody predicted. Consider adding 5-10% of the total expenses to give yourself a little buffer.

Provide Pampering For Free or at Cost

There are services you provide at your event that are meant to pamper your guests. I recommend that these types of services not be used to make a profit. Rather, they should be provided free of charge or at cost. They would include:

- Valet parking
- Coat check
- The bar
- Delivery of large auction items

Make Chairpersons Accountable

Once your budget is finalized, and each chairperson knows how much he or she has to spend, don't retire your money-manager hat just yet. Hold your people responsible for staying within the budget by requiring periodic reports of what has been spent. Authorize only certain people to be able to write a check or use a credit card.

Require everybody to produce a receipt for everything purchased or rented. Encourage everyone to exhaust all possible In-kind services (3.1) or free resources before resorting to paying full price for anything. If the actual expenses are not in line with the budget, find out why.

If you are a 501(c)(3) non-profit organization, you are may be exempt from paying state sales tax. If so, furnish your tax-exempt number to everyone who has authorization to make purchases.

Add a new column to your Budget Spreadsheet (1.2). Name the new column "Actual". It is in this column that you will put actual expenses and revenue. After the event, you can analyze the spreadsheet and see how close your predictions were to the actual amounts. This spreadsheet will hold valuable information for the people who plan next year's event.

Involve the Accountant in Everything

Your organization should have an accountant and you should have full access to that person. The accountant should attend every meeting where money is discussed. He or she should be involved in everything that has to do with money: the budget, monitoring expenses, doing the bookkeeping, and the money part of the Post Event Evaluation (1.20). Every penny made and spent should be accounted for.

Don't Proceed Without a Budget

You might be tempted to skip the budget planning process. Don't do it. A realistic budget motivates people within your organization, and people within the community to whom you look for support. It also makes your fundraising event easier to manage because you know where you want to go and what is needed to get there. Also, if your fundraiser is an annual affair, each fundraising plan will get easier because of what you learned the year before, and you will be able to make more accurate predictions for each upcoming event.

1.3 Analyze last year's event scrapbook

If a Scrapbook (15.1) was compiled from last year's event you are fortunate. You won't have to reinvent the wheel. You have all sorts of records, lists, photos, and descriptions of what went right and what went wrong from the last event, making it easier to produce your event. By analyzing the last event, you're going to make your event bigger and better. Make sure a Scrapbook is compiled for YOUR event.

1.4 Set the date and time

Date

Steer around holidays, three-day weekends and school breaks. Many people leave town during these times. Consider school graduations, major community events, opening hunting and fishing days, and religious holidays at the same time you are considering holding your event that would cause your attendance to suffer.

Major sporting events can also steal potential guests. I was helping an organization that held their fundraiser on the same evening that their city's NBA basketball team was having a play-off game for the national championship. The organizers had no way of knowing that this conflict would arise when they planned the date of their event months earlier. They were worried that many of their invited guests would stay home and watch the game on TV.

They came up with a great idea. They sent out post cards announcing that the game would be projected on a huge screen during the event. The event went on as planned. The game was projected on a big screen next to the stage with the sound turned off. The guests were able to watch the game and enjoy the fundraiser at the same time.

Some organizations schedule events for the middle of the week so people who normally go out of town on the weekends can attend.

Time

The time of day to hold events that feature auctions is traditionally limited to afternoon or evening. There has been, however, quite a proliferation of breakfast fundraising events over the past few years. If your event is scheduled during a weekday evening, start at 5:30 p.m. because some people will come straight from work and will be hungry.

1.5   Set the theme and attire

Think about the ambiance you want to create at your event. Consider how you can use lighting, music, decorations, flowers, table cloth and place settings, centerpieces, ice carvings, foliage and plants, scenery, stage backdrops, candles, balloon arches, and party favors. The entrance to your event should be decorated to reflect your theme. Themes serve to give your event variety from year to year. Themes also unite a group of strangers. Possible themes include:

- Western
- Tropical island or Hawaiian
- Mardi-Gras
- Costume
- Fabulous 50's
- African safari
- Sports night
- Viva Las Vegas
- Medieval
- Oriental Odyssey
- Hollywood
- Come as you are

Possible attire:

- **Black Tie** – tuxedos and long cocktail dresses
- **Black Tie optional/invited** – optional dark suit for him and dressy evening separates for her
- **Creative Black Tie** – More trendy. Perhaps a black shirt for him and a long or short dress for her.
- **Semi-Formal** – dark suits and cocktail dresses
- **Business Formal** – same as semi-formal for him, tailored dress suits and dresses for her
- **Cocktail Attire** – dark suits and elegant dresses
- **Dressy Casual** – a dressed up version of casual. Trousers and sports coat for him. Dressy pants for her
- **Casual** – generally, anything goes
- **Festive Attire** – a holiday or more flashy look

You can also choose not to have a theme. Going without a theme can save on decorations and graphic design for your invitations and printed program. You would have to find something else to give your event variety from year to year. Perhaps you could focus on entertainment or the celebrities you invite.

1.6   Reserve a location

Outdoors or indoors? I conducted an auction outside at a ski resort on a winter day, so outdoors in the middle of winter might be a consideration for you. And then, maybe not. But I have attended many outdoor fundraisers in warm weather. Consider holding yours in a park, in an outdoor pavilion or under a big tent. Make sure accommodations are made for hot weather, such as water, shade and seating for everyone. Consider providing canopies for those wanting to get out of the hot sun.

If you plan an outside event and it rains, what are you going to do? Having a contingency plan is a must.

Sound systems (10.25) sound differently outside than inside. Voices easily heard indoors might get lost to the wind outdoors. Just be aware you might need to add one or more speakers to your sound system if your event is held outdoors.

Possible indoor venues include:

- Convention centers
- Libraries
- Hotels
- Churches
- Museums
- Night clubs or restaurants
- Boats (large ones)
- Airplane hangers
- School auditoriums or gymnasiums
- Warehouses
- Theaters

The list can go on. Reserve your location as far in advance as you can. Some venues require reservations more than a year in advance.

Some venues, such as hotels, hold multiple events at the same time. Find out what other events are planned in the same building at the same time as your event. Make sure it is not one so noisy that it will interrupt your event, such as a concert or a school dance. Also find out if any of the competing events will spill out into hallways where they may interfere with guests' access to your own event.

Whether your event is indoors or outdoors, there are some things to be considered before you put that deposit down. Get with your Party/Decorations/Entertainment Chair (10) and make a list of everything you will need for your event. Write it down. Keep in mind that some places require you to use their audio/visual equipment, extension cords, caterers, etc. Be sure to ask about the costs, restrictions and policies. And by all means, visit your short list of possible sites before making any final decisions.

Here is a secret to help you find a good place to hold your event. Contact your local Convention and Visitors Bureau. They know about places you can hold your event that you may not be aware of. They may also be able to help with your selection of service and equipment providers. To find the website of your Convention and Visitors Bureau, go to **www.LetsDoAnAuction.com/resources.htm.**

Did I mention to reserve your location early?

Also keep this in mind. You are planning a fundraiser. You have every right to ask for space, equipment and services to be donated. See In-kind services (3.1). If you cannot get what you want for free, try to negotiate a lower-than-normal fee. Here is a list of considerations when selecting a place to hold your event:

- **Space** – Is there enough space for everyone, tables, chairs, aisles, stage, audio/visual equipment, silent auction tables, bars, entertainers, etc.?
- **Extra rooms** – Will you need rooms for coat-check and volunteers? Will you need a secure room to lock up auction items, purses and other valuables? Will you need dressing rooms?
- **Obligation to pay** – Understand the deposit, payment, and cancellation policies. Also ask whether gratuities are mandatory or optional. Discuss insurance requirements.
- **Easy to find** – If it's not easy to find, provide a map with the invitation.
- **Travel time** – A long drive might discourage guests from coming.
- **Signage** – Will the venue be tricky enough to find that you will need signage to direct guests to your event, and where to park at your event?
- **Restrictions** – Ask what, if any, are their restrictions.
- **Services** – Understand the services provided by the facility and whether someone from the facility will be

on hand during the event. Does the facility have a list of suppliers they prefer to use?

- **Restrooms** – Can they handle all your guests without long waiting lines? Are they maintained with paper products and kept clean? Who pays for that?
- **Electricity** – Are there enough outlets? Are the outlets placed conveniently? Is there a danger of blowing a fuse with the lighting and sound equipment? Where is the fuse box? How do you reset the fuses?
- **Lighting** – Will you be able to adjust the lighting down for a PowerPoint presentation, and up for the live auction?
- **View impediments** – Are there posts or other obstacles that would obstruct anyone's view of the stage?
- **Acoustics** – Is there a bad echo in the room? I visited an auction once where the echo was so bad, that the Auctioneer actually gave up using the microphone. The echo was less distracting without the sound system. Of course without a sound system, only those sitting close the Auctioneer could hear very well.
- **Climate control** – Will you be able to control the heating in case it turns cold, and the air conditioning in case body heat from all your guests causes the temperature to rise to an uncomfortable level?
- **Accommodations for the disabled** – Can people in wheelchairs access all areas of the event including restrooms? Is the facility in compliance with the Americans with Disabilities Act (ADA)?
- **Renovation plans** – Will any renovations be going on during your event that will cause a disruption?
- **Tent heaters** – A warm day in a tent can turn cold at night. Will your guests be uncomfortable without a heat source?

- **Mosquitoes** – A warm day outside without bugs could turn into a feeding frenzy for bugs after the sun goes down.
- **Noise ordinances** – I once saw the police shut down the post-auction entertainment because the city ordinance said no noise after 10:00 pm. You might be able to get an Ordinance Variance to allow you to be noisy past the designated ordinance time. Check with your local and city governments for local and city noise ordinances and variances.
- **Other city ordinances** – Are there any other restrictions for a large gathering outside.
- **Sound system** – The house sound system may not be adequate. Don't assume it is or take anyone's word for it. *A good sound system is critical.* Listen to it and judge for yourself. Will you have to rent sound equipment from an outside source?
- **Video system** – Is there a good place to show your video or PowerPoint presentation?
- **Parking** – Is there enough parking for guests? Will there be a long walk for guests? Will guests feel safe in the parking lot? Will you have to arrange a shuttle bus or valet parking? Will you need to distribute parking validations so your guests won't have to pay to park?
- **Delivery access** – Will you be able to drive trucks close for easy delivery or will you have to carry food, equipment, and other items by hand over a long distance? Will you have unlimited access to loading zones, or will there be strict time restrictions? Who else will require the use of your loading zones?
- **Bad weather plan** – if your venue is outside, will there be somewhere for guests to escape a rain storm?
- **Portable flooring on top of grass** – for those wearing high heals or those who are disabled.
- **Alcohol** – Check the laws for serving alcoholic drinks.

- **Insurance** – What if a guest trips and gets hurt?
- **Placement of decorations and banners** – Are there any restrictions for decorating or hanging banners? Are there hooks or otherwise good places on which to hang banners?
- **Setup start time** – How early in the day can you take over the facility to get things ready? I worked with an organization that was surprised to discover they couldn't have the room they needed until 2:00 p.m. The event was to start at 5:00. Be sure you have plenty of time to set up.
- **Freight elevator** – How big and how many? Will it be adequate?
- **Maximum room capacity** – Do not exceed the fire code maximum capacity or you may be fined.
- **Zoning regulations** – Will the city allow you to hold a gathering there? Erect a tent?
- **Facilities for food preparation** – Are they adequate?
- **Distractions** – Will your guests be distracted by a noisy street or hallway, a clanky heating system, a nearby racetrack, or another function going on next door?
- **Tables and chairs** – Are tables and chairs included with the venue or will you have to rent them from an outside provider? Are table coverings included with the tables?
- **Emergency exits** – Are they clearly marked? Be careful not to obstruct them.
- **Security** – Is security provided?
- **Necessary items** – Some venues, such as hotels and conference centers will require you to use (and pay extra for) items you may need. Find out in advance what they are. These items can include:
  - Tables and chairs
  - Table coverings
  - Stage and podium
  - Curtains

- o Sound equipment
- o Extension cords
- o Easels
- o Extra lighting such as spotlights
- o Projectors and screens
- o Technical staff to setup and handle problems with the equipment
- **Get it in writing** – Make sure you get **all** agreements in writing before you put down a deposit. Do not assume any verbal agreement will happen the way you expect.
- **Get references** – Find out what other groups have recently used the facility and call them before you sign anything.
- **Get contact information** – Get phone numbers and cell numbers of people for questions before and during the event. **Note:** always carry contact information on all of your vendors on the day of your event so you don't have to waste time looking up phone numbers when you need them.

1.7   Sit-down vs. stand-up audiences

Stand-up audiences are typically noisier than sit-down audiences. Sit-down audiences are better suited for Fund-a-Program (12.23). Stand-up audiences require that the Auctioneer stand on a platform or stage in order to see the entire audience.

Personally I prefer sit-down audiences because they are usually quieter and pay attention to the Auctioneer longer. But I've conducted many successful auctions in front of stand-up crowds.

You should provide some seating for stand-up audiences because there will be people who don't want to or cannot stand for long periods of time.

1.8 Reserved seating vs. open seating

Is it better to have reserved seating or open seating? Reserved seating means a reserved table. Guests can sit in any vacant seat at his or her reserved table. The number of seats at a reserved table should be an even number, usually eight or ten to accommodate couples. Open seating means first-come-first-serve; any table is fair game. Let's look at some advantages and disadvantages of each.

Reserved Seating

Advantages: Reserved seating makes guests feel important. They know they can arrive at their table anytime and have a seat vacant and waiting for them. Guests don't have to worry about someone taking their seat if they need to get up and go somewhere. Guests who are known to bid a lot can be assigned to sit at tables closer to the stage. Reserved seating is best for finding people to notify them that they won a silent auction item. With reserved seating, you can determine if a head table is needed and who will sit there.

Disadvantages: There's more work involved for your Reservations Chairperson. Seating charts need to be made and guests need to be assigned tables. Table-number cards need to be printed and displayed on each table. Ushers may be needed to help people find their assigned tables. A large map of the room (8.3) displaying the location of tables may be helpful for guests who get lost easily.

Open Seating

Advantages: There's less work for your Reservations Chairperson. If you are not using reservations or bid numbers (1.9), then a registration table (8.8) at the entrance of the event might not be necessary. You might, however, want to have a table set up to receive and sell tickets.

Disadvantages: Guests miss out on the warm fuzzy feeling that reserved seating gives them. People must arrive early to get the seats they want. Guests need to come up with a method to stake out the seats they have claimed and risk losing their seats if they go anywhere. You lose the advantage of being able to pre-sell entire tables unless you reserved some tables and pronounce them off-limits to the masses with a big RESERVED sign. Open seating means it will be nearly impossible to track individuals down to notify them about their silent auction winnings.

If you want to know my opinion, I'm all for reserved seating for the reasons stated above. But then, I don't have to make all the arrangements.

1.9 To use bid numbers or not

Bid numbers are numbers that you assign to your guests and are used in place of names to identify bidders.

Is it better to use bid numbers or not? I hear this question a lot. As the Auctioneer, I have a personal stake in the decision. So I have an opinion. See if you agree with me.

When to Use Bid Numbers

Use bid numbers when you want people to bid on the silent auction items using their bid numbers for identification. It is faster for guests to simply write down their bid numbers rather than the alternative – their names. But more importantly, it is usually easier to read numbers than names when identifying the winners of the silent auction items.

Use bid numbers when you want to identify the winning bidders of live auction items by number. The winning bidder holds up his or her bid number and the Auctioneer calls out, "Sold to bidder number 90". The Clerk (12.18) records the numbers.

Use bid numbers when you are going to do Fund-a-Program (12.23) or sell Sponsorships (12.24). The

Auctioneer will read the many bid numbers that people hold up in the air.

The disadvantage of using bid numbers is the time and effort it takes to assign bid numbers to guests. You'll also need to write the bid number down on the back of each printed program or on a bid card of some kind to give to each guest. The guests must keep their bid numbers close at hand so they can use their bid numbers to bid on silent and live auction items.

When Not to Use Bid Numbers

Don't use bid numbers when you want people to bid on silent auction items by writing their names. Sometimes friends enjoy bidding against each other. If people write down their names, then they know who they are bidding against.

If you don't use bid numbers, you will have to assign someone to get the names of all the winning bidders during the live auction. The Auctioneer and Bid Spotters (12.16) can identify the location of the winning bidders to whoever gathers the information.

If you don't use bid numbers, it will be impossible to do Fund-a-Program or sell Sponsorships. How would the Auctioneer identify each donor unless the Auctioneer knew each donor by name?

Have you guessed which side of the debate I'm on? Sometimes I conduct auctions where no bid numbers are used. After selling each item I have to direct someone to the table of the winning bidder. It's a small distraction, but nevertheless a distraction and it takes a little extra time. I vote for bid numbers.

Bid Number Essentials

If you decide to use bid numbers, PLEASE READ THIS! The Auctioneer needs to be able to read every bid number from the stage. Therefore, it is important that each bid number be displayed large enough to be read from the stage.

Each bid number should be **black on a white background**, written horizontally, left to right. Limit the number of digits to be four or less. I've seen bid numbers where the table number is part of the bid number. For example, bid number 1203 would mean table 12, bidder number 03. This can be a handy way to locate the winner of a silent or live auction item.

Refrain from using letters. Some letters sound too much alike when the Auctioneer reads the bid numbers for the Clerk to record e.g. B P D E G.

The importance of using easy-to-read bid numbers was driven home to me when I did an auction where the numbers were written with a thin felt-tip pen on a green background. Six numbers were written vertically, top-to-bottom and each number was no taller than two inches. Some numbers were only an inch tall. I could only read the winning bidder's bid number by walking (or running in most cases) right up to the table where the bidder was sitting. This was in the large grand ballroom of a hotel, where over 800 people sat around tables. It caused the auction to slow down while I awkwardly weaved around tables to get close enough to read winning bid numbers. The awkwardness was especially apparent when we sold Sponsorships (12.24), and I had to read the many bid numbers that guests held up.

Here is a way to plan how big to make your bid numbers. After you have reserved the venue, have someone count how many steps it is from the stage area to where the farthest bidder will be sitting or standing. Then, sometime before the bid numbers are produced, have someone step off that distance and display various sizes of bid numbers. Make sure the bid numbers you use are large and bold enough to see from that distance. Or - just make your bid numbers six inches tall and very bold, on a white background.

Another rule of thumb is, if you can cover up most of the bid number with your fist, it's too small.

1.10   Decide on the ticket price

Deciding on the price to charge per admission ticket can be a daunting task. You don't want to charge too much or it might scare people off. You don't want to charge too little or people might feel it's not worth attending.

Try this exercise. See if it doesn't at least give you some prices to think about. Gather your chairpersons together and do this as a group. Read the following statements and follow the instructions.

1. Write down the cost of tickets you know other organizations charge for their events. Compare your event to theirs and make appropriate adjustments up or down. Write down that ticket price.
2. Write down the most you think the people on your Mailing List (7.1) would pay for a ticket if they learned you were going to have an event that was fun, filled with entertainment, gifts, good food, show-business, celebrities, personal attention and other forms of pampering, AND give them an opportunity to help support your cause, AND they would have fun bidding at your silent and live auctions. Of course they would learn about all this from your Publicity (5) and Invitations (7).
3. Some professional fundraisers say that revenue from ticket sales should cover the cost of the event – the venue, the dinner, drinks, printing, postage, etc. Then, from the moment your first guest walks through the door and buys a ticket for the drawing, or bids on a silent auction item, you are making money. Figure ticket price with the following formula:

$$\frac{\text{Total expenses}}{\text{Number of guests you expect to attend}} = \text{Ticket price}$$

4. Having come up with three possible ticket prices, decide on a tentative ticket price. Sleep on it for a few nights – maybe a few weeks if you have the time. See how it looks in your publicity and invitation drafts. Then make a final decision and go with it.

1.11 Invite your celebrity guest

Having a celebrity at your event gives your guests an experience they probably would not get anywhere else. It falls within the category of pampering and entertaining your guests.

A celebrity can be a TV or movie star, a popular entertainer, a local radio or TV personality, a government official like a governor, mayor or senator, a well-known CEO of a corporation, or a local or national popular sports figure. Invite your celebrity as far in advance as possible. Then have a backup plan because celebrities are notorious for backing out at the last minute.

Arrange for someone to meet your celebrity upon arrival. Find out how they intend to arrive and about what time. I was at a fundraiser where the celebrity arrived by helicopter. No one was there to greet him. So I pretended to be the welcoming committee.

Also, arrange for someone to accompany your celebrity throughout the evening. It makes the celebrity look and feel more important.

Don't spend a lot of money to have a big-name celebrity at your event. If you have to pay for their first-class air fare, limousine, hotel suite and all their food, the return on your investment is probably not worth it. If you know that a certain celebrity is going to be in town, ask if it would be possible to drop by and make a cameo appearance.

What's better than a celebrity at your event? Many celebrities. A room sprinkled with local TV and radio personalities, sports figures, political people and entertainers can add pizzazz to your event. Put your celebrity to work:

- Have a VIP reception before the general reception where guests who pay a little extra for tickets can meet and talk with your celebrity. VIPs can also be major donors, sponsors, etc.
- Have your celebrity greet people as they enter the event. Another person such as a member of the board or executive director should greet people with the celebrity. Keep the guests moving. No time to talk when greeting.
- Have your celebrity describe the live auction items (12.14). Provide a script.
- Invite your celebrity to act as Silent Auction Emcee (11.1). Provide a list of announcements to be made and an assistant to give help or answer questions.
- If your celebrity is an entertainer, have him/her/them entertain.

You can also use your celebrity to help raise money. See Procure Items for Silent and Live Auctions (4.4).

1.12 Prepare an event fact sheet

Your event fact sheet is a summary of your event. It will go to all staff, chairs, volunteers and the media. All the information goes on one sheet of paper. It is used to answer most of the questions that anyone will ask about your event. Your Event Fact Sheet should be easy to read at a glance and contain the following information.

- Date
- Time
- Location
- Theme
- Attire
- Ticket price
- How much you intend to raise
- The compelling reason to raise the money

- Celebrity guest
- How much you raised last year
- Where last year's money went

When volunteers talk with potential donors and guests, they will share the information on the Event Fact Sheet. The fact sheet will go to the media along with the press release to give journalists a summary of your event at a glance.

1.13 Draft an agenda for the event

Here is an example of an agenda as it appears in the printed program:

5:30 pm	Social hour, hors d'oeuvres, and silent auction
6:50 pm	Silent auction closes
7:00 pm	Welcome by emcee
7:10 pm	Dinner
8:00 pm	Live auction

…but the agenda in your notes may look something like this:

8:00 a.m.	Setup begins
2:00 p.m.	Dinner orchestra setup and rehearsal Caterer begins to set up tables
2:30 p.m.	Centerpieces arrive and volunteers put them on tables
4:00 p.m.	Joint volunteer briefing Sound system is setup and tested
4:15 p.m.	Volunteers split into areas of responsibility for additional training Live auction rehearsal with Auctioneer, Bid Spotters, Clerks and Runners
4:45 p.m.	Volunteer buffet Photographer sets up

5:00 p.m.	Quartet arrives and sets up
5:15 p.m.	Security person arrives in uniform
5:30 p.m.	Registration volunteers are set-up and ready for guests to arrive
	Greeters are at the entrance to greet guests
	Quartet begins to perform
	Volunteers begin selling tickets for drawing
	Volunteer begins to model the jewelry in the live auction
	Photographer begins taking portraits of guests
6:00 p.m.	Silent Auction Emcee begins to make announcements
6:54 p.m.	First section of silent auction closes
6:57 p.m.	Second section of silent auction closes
7:00 p.m.	Third and last section of silent auction closes
	Dinner emcee invites guests to be seated for dinner
	Quartet packs up
	Dinner orchestra begins to play
7:10 p.m.	Dinner begins to be served
	Volunteers continue to sell tickets for drawings
	Model continues to model jewelry in live auction
7:15 p.m.	Volunteers begin to notify silent auction winners
	Cashier volunteers man the Cashier table.
7:45 p.m.	Dinner emcee introduces Celebrity emcee
	...who thanks guests for coming and gives short emotional appeal
	Desert and coffee begin to be served
7:50 p.m.	Dinner emcee introduces Board Chairperson
	...who recognizes sponsors
7:55 p.m.	5-minute video is shown
8:00 p.m.	Live auction volunteers take their places
	Dinner emcee introduces celebrity emcee (as Item Describer)
	...who introduces Auctioneer. Auction begins.

	Drawings are held at predetermined intervals
9:00 p.m.	Auction ends
	Orchestra resumes entertainment
	Cleanup begins
10:00 p.m.	Orchestra packs up

The agenda is a living document, subject to change up to the last day. I don't see agendas followed to the minute very often. Schedules have a tendency to run late. In order to keep things on schedule as best you can, think of all the things that could go wrong to throw your schedule off, and plan what to do to prevent those bad things from happening.

One of the most common things to go wrong is a speaker or entertainer taking too long. Make sure they know how long they have to speak or perform and how important it is to stick with the schedule.

Another common problem is trying to move a large group of people from one place to another. For example, asking everyone to move from the silent auction/reception area to the eating area, or from the eating area to the live auction area. Moving large groups of people usually takes longer than planned.

There are some creative ways to announce that the crowd is invited to move to another area. Consider using a trumpeter along with a loudspeaker announcement. How about a mariachi band that winds its way through the silent auction area and leads the guests to the dining area? I've seen volunteers wandering through the crowd ringing little bells to get people moving.

It's better if the silent auction, the dinner, the live auction, and the entertainment all take place in the same room.

The live auction should start around the time dessert is being served, because after eating desert, some people start thinking about leaving. If they eat desert while the auction is going, it helps to keep them entertained.

At 10:00 pm, people will start to leave regardless of whether or not the live auction is over.

Event Chair

A good time to have the last drawing is right after the live auction in order to keep people from wandering off. You must be present to win, of course.

Post-Auction Dance

It is my experience that most people are ready to leave after the live auction. So if you plan to have a post-auction dance, you may only have the clean-up committee attending. Now don't everyone who has had a successful post-auction dance email me. I have seen exceptions. One exception is when a majority of your guests are single (non-married) people. They are likely to stay for a post-auction dance. If you do have a dance, start as soon as possible after the live auction. The longer you wait, the more people you stand to lose.

Entertainment

Short entertainment should happen during dinner. Entertainment that takes longer should happen after the live auction. Use an entertainer to keep people in their seats during the auction by scheduling the entertainer to perform after the auction. Guests will believe that the entertainer is part of their admission price and will want to stay for the entertainment.

Don't Divide the Live Auction into Segments

What about auctioning something off and then having some entertainment and then auctioning a little more and then doing something else for a while and coming back to auction off some more stuff? I've done auctions like this. "Gather 'round, folks. It's time again to auction off some more things. I hope you remember that thrill of bidding we felt the last time we got together. Let's see if we can capture that mood again." You can tell I'm not a fan of dividing the auction into segments. In my opinion, it causes the auction to lose momentum. It's also hard to move a large group of people back to the location of your live auction.

Social Hour Entertainment

Here are some ideas for entertainment or activities to happen during social hour:

- A VIP social hour to precede the general social hour. Make sure your celebrity guest attends.
- Silent auction
- Sell things at your event mini-store (10.37) to raise money
- Hors d'oeuvres
- Live background music
- Magician
- Mime
- Trampoline exhibition
- Quartet, guitar players, harpist, mini-band
- Displays to heighten guests' awareness of your cause
- Alcoholic drinks served
- Non-alcoholic drinks served
- Games such as:
- Darts and balloons
- Beanbag toss
- Baseball toss
- Basketball toss
- Horseshoe toss
- Golf ball putting
- Other carnival-type games
- Casino games
- Sell raffle tickets for the drawing – where raffle tickets are illegal because of gambling restrictions, offer tickets for a suggested donation amount.
- Use a photographer to take pictures of guests, using a background that goes with the theme. Use digital photography and print the pictures at the event.
- Use a photographer to wander around during the social hour taking pictures of guests, using digital

photography and printing the pictures at the event. Display all the pictures on a display board for all to see. Invite the guests to take the picture of themselves home with them.

Dinner Entertainment

Here are some ideas to do during dinner:

- Short entertainment – singers, dancers
- Entertaining speaker
- Professional comedian (I've seen comedians crash and burn at fundraisers because guests continue to socialize. So try to get someone who is good at keeping the crowd's attention.)
- Short video or PowerPoint presentation
- Prize drawing
- Award presentations
- Present a community service award
- Emotional appeal (1.18)
- No entertainment. Just allow guests to enjoy a quiet meal and visit with each other.

1.14 Select and secure chairpersons

I have worked with Executive Directors who have single-handedly organized the entire event. By the end of the event, they are pretty much frazzled, stressed out and over-worked. Some of them left the organization soon after they were done. Putting on your event can and should be fun. And when you are done, you should feel a high degree of satisfaction. You should be able to share that joy with others who have worked for the same outcome and with whom you have formed a bond of friendship.

So get some help. Ask board members to suggest people they know who might help. Call company CEOs and ask if they know anyone who would chair a committee. Ask former contributors to help. They just might be flattered that you would ask them for something other than money.

In any case, be prepared to answer the Two Burning Questions discussed in Catch the Vision (1.1) which are:

1. How much are you trying to raise?
2. What is the money going to be used for?

The Chairs need to buy into the answers to these questions and believe they are attainable.

The point is, don't think you can single-handedly do a better job than you could with an army of chairpersons helping you. Share the load. Spread the joy.

Honorary Chairperson

Don't overlook the value of an honorary chairperson. Their sole purpose is to lend credibility to your event and allow you to throw their name around to get donations and guests. They must be someone who is well known and respected within the community. They won't do any work other than make a small speech at your event.

1.15 Decide on donor incentives

If you want someone to donate something to you, you've got be willing to give something back. In other words, you've got to be willing to promote the donor's company. Procurement should be a win/win proposition. The larger the donation the more you should be willing to give. Consider these ideas in exchange for donations:

- Recognition in the printed program and/or during the live auction as a donor
- Quarter, half, full-page, or double-page ad in the printed program

- Signage or banner with name and logo displayed at the event
- Their name announced during dinner or during the live auction as a contributor
- A framed Certificate of Appreciation to hang where their customers can see
- Name and logo in the newsletter, in promotional advertising, and/or on a poster outside the main entrance to the event
- Tickets to the event
- Tickets to the VIP reception to be held before the general reception where guests can meet and talk with the guest celebrity
- Their own table at the event
- Guaranteed seating near the stage
- Permission to set up a display or booth at the event
- Allow the donor to benefit from your mailing list. I'm not suggesting you give them your mailing list. First you approve their promotional material. It might say that this special offer is made especially for friends of your organization. They stuff the envelopes and provide the postage. *You* provide the mailing labels and drop them in the mail. *You* control the mailing.
- Have you been to a movie where slides promoting businesses were projected onto the big screen before the show began? Why do you suppose they do that? They do that because people will pay for that kind of advertising. Why not offer the same benefit at your event? Project some PowerPoint revolving slides onto a big screen during dinner to promote your donors and sponsors.

Some organizations hold thank-you luncheons for donors and sponsors after the event to promote and continue their relationships. Remember, building relationships is an important part of fundraising. You want to be able to ask for, and get help from the same donors and sponsors year after year.

With your incentives, you give businesses another way to gain visibility in the community, while supporting a good cause at the same time. Make sure that everyone knows what incentives they can use when going after donations.

1.16 Provide for short lines

One of the ways to pamper guests is to do whatever is necessary to avoid having them wait in lines. People do not like to wait in lines. This book shows ways to reduce long lines. Make sure your Chairs are aware of the common places where long lines can occur. They can occur at the:

- Registration table (8.2)
- Entrance to the event (10.8)
- Bars (10.11)
- Restrooms (10.32)
- Buffet tables (10.16)
- Cashier table (13.1)
- Valet parking – leaving the event (10.2)

1.17 Arrange for a VIP to greet guests

You should start making people feel important the moment they step into your event. You will recall that making people feel important is the first of **The Four Objectives of a Successful Fundraiser**. If guests were to be greeted by a VIP-type person upon entering your event, you would be off to a good start.

A VIP can be a director of the board, member of the board, Executive Director or celebrity. A celebrity can be a TV or movie star, a local radio or TV personality, a government official such as a governor, mayor, congressman, senator, or county commissioner. A popular sports figure makes a good celebrity as well.

Another idea is to have someone in costume greet guests. If your organization is a theatre, ballet or symphony, have one or two of the performers dressed in their costumes greet guests. Have the director or the conductor greet guests. If you're a school, have the principal be a greeter.

You should have someone accompany your VIP, introduce the VIP, and keep the line moving. People love to talk to VIPs – and that will stop guests from entering your event. Advise the VIP greeter to refrain from engaging in chit-chat as long as there are people waiting to come in.

1.18   Arrange for an emotional appeal

The second objective in **The Four Objectives of a Successful Fundraiser** is to get your guests to gain a desire to support your cause. One of the best ways I've found to do that is to make an emotional appeal.

What? An emotional appeal is a short speech, video presentation or PowerPoint presentation that explains why it is so important to raise money. It should be emotional. Thus the name: emotional appeal. It should cause everyone in the audience to gain a desire to support your cause if they haven't already. It should leave everyone a little misty-eyed if it involves helping people. It should give everyone a good reason to bid high.

Why? We want people to bid on items not just because they want the items, but because they want to support your cause. Bidders who feel strongly about supporting your cause often bid higher than the item's retail value. How much higher? I once sold a bicycle worth about $4,500 for $29,000. Why did it go for so much? Well, **The Four Objectives of a Successful Fundraiser** had certainly been achieved. But the handful of people bidding on the bike felt so strongly about supporting the organization's cause, they felt good about bidding the bike way up.

Who? If the emotional appeal is given by way of a short speech, the person giving the speech should be someone well acquainted with the program. He or she should be someone with a passion for what your organization does. Someone who has benefited from your organization often makes a good presenter. Whoever it is should have plenty of advance notice.

How long? Video and PowerPoint presentations shouldn't take more than about six or seven minutes. I've discovered guests prefer to move on after six or seven minutes. If a person is to give a speech, two or three minutes is good, six or seven minutes is okay only if that person is really captivating the audience. People who have benefited from the organization tend to talk longer than others. Make sure your Emotional Appeal Giver is aware of the time limit.

When? Arrange for the emotional appeal to happen just before the live auction begins. Right after the emotional appeal, introduce the Auctioneer.

1.19 Motivate and retain volunteers

Usually, volunteers need to be motivated unless they are going golfing or leaving on a vacation, in which case, they are self-motivated. It is important to know how to motivate because if volunteers are not properly groomed and motivated, they will disappear one by one (or maybe all at once) but they will disappear. Following is a three-step motivation formula:

1. Get people caught up in your vision.
2. Set measurable goals.
3. Use incentives, feedback on performance, praise and recognition.

Get People Caught Up in Your Vision

Your volunteers need to "catch the vision" (1.1) just like you did. They need to feel your passion and understand why you have such a profound desire to help this organization. They need to have an experience that shows them how their efforts are going to make a difference in

51

peoples' lives – the people that your organization serves. Your volunteers need to form a bond with you and with the other volunteers by sharing a common vision.

Provide an opportunity for your volunteers to see, first hand, what your organization does to help people. Go on a tour. Meet and talk with people who your organization is helping. Let them hear from staff members and board members who are dedicated to serving in your organization. The Volunteer Orientation (2.3) would be the best place to start the ball rolling.

Set Measurable Goals

Goals motivate. Especially if the people who you want to motivate have a hand in setting the goals. Set team goals and individual goals. Goals must be specific and measurable. None of this "procure as many items as we can" stuff. I want to see numbers!

Incentives

Let volunteers know from the beginning that you are going to let them know how they are doing. If people know they will be recognized for achieving goals or winning a competition, they tend to work harder. Consider offering a prize to the team or individual who, since the last meeting:

1. Reached their goal
2. Procured the most items
3. Procured the most expensive item
4. Invited the most people who attend
5. Worked the most hours
6. Received the most "no's"
7. Made the most contacts
8. Got the worst excuse for not donating or attending

Feedback on Performance

A powerful motivator of people is immediate feedback on results. It is why beginning golfers have a hard time keeping their heads down until they follow through with their swing. They crave immediate feedback on their performance and want to see where that ball is going.

Your volunteers need feedback on how they are doing. They need to be praised and recognized for achieving their assigned tasks. As their leader, you need to know the results of their performance so you can deliver praise and recognition – or encouragement and support.

As people are learning to be good performers, they need more feedback. Then as they gain more experience, you can cut down the frequency of giving feedback because getting their own feedback will motivate them. They still need the information, but it doesn't need to be delivered by you.

Have your volunteers keep track of how many people they contact, and how many of those contacts ended in success. Whether it is procuring items or inviting people, accumulate individual and team statistics by phone or email and keep good records.

Praise

In their best-selling book, *The One Minute Manager*, co-authors Ken Blanchard and Spencer Johnson show praising to be a necessary part of effective leadership. They teach that the key to developing people is to catch them doing something right.

People who feel good about themselves produce more good results. People produce better when they feel appreciated. Catching people doing something right motivates and gives people energy.

Praise progress. The power of praise comes from the knowledge that someone took the time to notice the achievement, seek out the volunteer responsible and personally deliver the praise in a timely manner. A quick phone call, a note mailed, or an email doesn't take long but can have a lasting positive effect.

Praise is done in a one on one situation, where recognition (discussed below) is done in front of a group. To catch people doing something right, you must pay close attention to their activities by:

- Having volunteers keep records of their progress
- Having volunteers send progress reports to you on a regular basis

Consider the following four steps when praising your volunteers:

Step 1. Praise should be given as soon after the performance as possible. Pay a visit or make a phone call.

Step 2. Tell the person what they did right. Be specific: "You got some great items donated. That TV is an incredible item and those tickets to the basketball game... on the 10th row - how did you accomplish that?" Don't say, "You're doing a super job." That's being too general, and you should be specific in this step.

Step 3. Share your feelings. Tell the person how good you feel about what they did: "That makes me feel good. We're making some great progress. I'm glad you're on our team."

Step 4. Encourage more of the same: "Keep up the good work." Now you can be more general: "You're doing a super job."

Recognition

Too often, the only time volunteers get any attention is when they make a mistake, and when they do well, nothing is said. Volunteers need to know that their contributions are noticed and appreciated. Recognition improves volunteers' self-esteem, which results in increased pride and productivity.

Recognition is usually done in a meeting attended by a team or the entire group of volunteers. Recognition can be given to a team or to individuals in the group. People should be recognized close to the time the achievement is realized, so periodic volunteer parties (meetings with food) are recommended.

The Event Chairperson should tell the group specifically why an individual is being recognized, and how that performance affects the fundraiser. Recognition can be a good source of motivation and should include a gift such as:

- Lunch with the Event Chairperson or a board member
- A balloon bouquet
- A gift certificate for a movie, eatery, round of golf, car wash, etc.
- A write-up about their achievement in the newsletter – photo included
- The "gold nugget award" – paint a rock gold
- Have your picture taken with the celebrity guest the night of the event
- A framed certificate of appreciation
- Two tickets for seats at the event
- Baseball cap or tee-shirt with the organization's logo on it
- Bonus tickets to be put into the drawing at the post-event party
- Recognition for their efforts at the event

Teach your chairpersons how to motivate because they will take up where you leave off. Remind your chairpersons to train their volunteers well, and never assume their volunteers understand their assignments without having been properly shown. And I mean shown – not just told. Volunteers who do not feel comfortable with their assignments will become former volunteers. Written instructions are helpful to remind the volunteers after they have received personal training.

1.20   Prepare a post-event evaluation

The Post-Event Evaluation is a tool that will help the next Event Chairperson prepare for the next event. It will be included in the Scrapbook (15.1) that will be presented to the next Event Chairperson. The Post-Event Evaluation should be completed within 15 days of the conclusion of the event while it is still fresh in everyone's mind. By analyzing the Post-Event Evaluation, the next Event Chairperson should have a good understanding of what went right so he or she can accentuate the good, and what went wrong, to avoid repeating the same mistakes.

Mail Survey to Guests

Don't guess how your guests felt about your event. Ask them. Send out a short survey on a post card. If you do not want to send one to every guest, send one to a cross section of your guests. The postcard should be self-addressed and include postage. You can enclose the postcard with your thank-you note (14.1). Here is a survey example:

Your comments about our Star Bright Gala are valuable to us and will be considered when planning our next event. Please answer this short survey and drop this postcard in the mail.

1 being the worst and 5 being the best:
How did you like the location?   1 2 3 4 5
How did you like the food?   1 2 3 4 5
How did you like the entertainment?   1 2 3 4 5
How did you like the Auctioneer?   1 2 3 4 5
What did you particularly like or dislike?

Create a Post-Event Evaluation form (suggested questions are below) and give one to each chairperson. Have each chairperson fill out the portions of the evaluation that relate to their responsibilities and return it to you. Combine all the information into one Post-Event Evaluation. Another option would be to hold a post-event meeting with all your chairpersons. Chairpersons should be prepared to present answers to the questions that fall under their individual responsibilities.

The purpose of the Post-Event Evaluation is to make next year's event even more successful than this year's event. It will also help the new Event Chairperson to organize the next event without having to "reinvent the wheel". Here are some possible topics to be included in the Post-Event Evaluation:

What went well?

What were the problems we faced? How could we have avoided them?

Donors:

- Who were the donors?
- Who were new donors compared to last year?
- Who were return donors from last year?
- Who were the biggest donors?

The party:

- How was the venue?
- Was the date a good choice?
- Did the event conflict with someone else's event?
- Were guests comfortable?
- How was the sound system?
- How well did the emcee perform?
- How was the food?
- How was the entertainment?
- How were the restrooms?
- How was the bar?
- Who made the centerpieces and what did they look like? Include pictures.
- How long did guests have to wait in the registration line?
- How long did guests have to wait in the check-out line?
- Were there enough volunteers?
- Did the volunteers perform well? Was training adequate?

Guests – compare to last year if possible (use numbers and percent increase or decrease):

- How many guests?
- How many guests were new?
- How many guests returned from last year?
- Who were your biggest buyers?

- Were there any big bidders from last year that did not attend this year?
- How many people who reserved seats did not show up?
- At what point did people start leaving to go home?
- Who purchased tables?
- How many guests got in for free?
- Were there any complaints from guests?
- Were there any praises from guests?

Silent and Live Auctions:

- What were the best selling items?
- What were the worst selling items?
- How was the emotional appeal? (1.18)
- What percent of retail value did the items sell for?
- How did the Auctioneer do? Would you use the same one again?

Financial Spreadsheet – compare to last year if possible AND compare with Budget (1.2)

- What did we raise from each income source?
  Single ticket sales
  Cash contributions
  Sponsors
  Table purchases
  Drawing
  Sale of centerpieces
  Silent auction
  Live auction
  Fund-a-Program
  Mini-store
- How did our actual revenue and expenses compare with the budget?
- What percent of the total revenue did each income source produce? This is important because it will tell

you what your top sources of income were and what your bottom sources of income were. Did 80% of your effort go into producing 20% of your income? If so, you may want to rethink where you expend your effort next time. Look at your top money producing sources. Perhaps you should focus more on increasing those sources of revenue next time.

- What were the expenses?
- What were the surprise expenses?
- What was the net profit?
- Did we reach our goal?
- How much publicity or media awareness did we get from Radio? From TV? From a feature article in a local newspaper or magazine (5.3)?

1.21   Conduct the post-event party

The post-event party is held to bring together everyone that helped make this event possible. That would include:

- All chairpersons
- Staff
- Organization leadership
- Board members
- Volunteers
- Auctioneer

By now, everyone who has worked to produce your event has formed friendships among each other, and hopefully, developed a desire to continue to help your cause. This party is held to show appreciation for everyone's help and make everyone feel good about the sacrifices they made to make this event possible. And you want them to do it again for the next event.

Preparing to put on an event is like being pregnant: There is a lot of planning and hard work. The event itself is like giving birth: Lots of stress and worry and the pain of solving unforeseen problems. That's why you never ask a chairperson if they might help again next year during the event. It's like asking a mother giving birth if she plans to have more kids.

But after the event, when there is no pressure, and everyone is happy the event is behind them, and most have forgotten how "bad it hurt", then we party so everyone's last impression of the event is a positive one.

If you don't want to spend any money on food, make it a potluck. Here are some things you can do at the post-event party to show your appreciation:

- Make sure there is lots of good food and drink.
- Give out certificates of appreciation or plaques of recognition.
- Give out hats, tee-shirts or other gifts.
- Have drawings and give away some fun stuff.
- Get feedback on what went well and what didn't.
- Announce the amount of money raised.
- Show slides that the photographer took on a continuous revolving PowerPoint presentation. Sometimes people who work at the event never see the event. Give people a picture of themselves working as part of an award.
- Announce who has accepted the responsibility of being the next Event Chairperson.

1.22   Event management software

Event management software is software that you load onto your computer (or your network of computers) to help you keep track of, and manage, all the information pertaining to your event. It also allows you to recall and compare information from past events.

If you are going to have an annual fundraiser, you need to keep track of volunteers, donors and guests from year to year. Event management software is good at doing that. Event management software can keep track of:

- Volunteers
- Donors
- Items and services procured
- Packaged items and services
- A mailing list of potential guests
- Guests in attendance
- Winning bidders and their purchases

Event management software has advantages and disadvantages:

Advantages

- Reports are easy to produce and can be filtered and sorted in a variety of ways.
- Some software allows you to produce donor slips, printed programs and bid sheets.
- Specific information only takes a few seconds to find.

Disadvantages:

- A basic understanding of computers is necessary.
- It is required to have a computer on which to run the software – a laptop computer will be easier to transport than a desk-top computer.
- There is the cost of the software which varies depending on the software's features.

To see a list of event management software, go to **www.LetsDoAnAuction.com/resources.htm**.

2. Volunteers Chair

2.1 Determine number of volunteers needed

The best way to determine how many volunteers you will need and what tasks they will perform is to ask all the chairpersons for their requirements. Plan ahead. Determine the tasks before you conduct your volunteer orientation (2.3). Make sure to ask the chairpersons to attend your volunteer orientation.

2.2 Recruit volunteers

The first place to look for volunteers is to contact the volunteers that helped you at your last fundraiser. If they were made to feel important, developed a desire to support your cause, and had fun, then chances are they will want to help again. If they didn't feel important or didn't develop a desire to support your cause, or didn't have fun, well, you've got your work cut out for you – so make sure they get treated right this year.

There are people who wonder, from time to time, how they can get involved as a volunteer for a non-profit organization. They are just waiting for the right opportunity. They are waiting to be asked. Here are some possible places to find volunteers.

- Use your board members as a resource. Ask them for names of people who they think would be interested in helping. Then call them.
- Use your staff and chairpersons as a resource. Ask them to help recruit volunteers.
- Ask volunteers to suggest names of friends or family members who might be willing to help.
- Ask people who have benefited from you organization's services. If you are a school, ask

teachers and substitute teachers to help. If your organization helps fight a disease, ask former patients. If your organization helps children, ask their parents to help as volunteers.

- Contact a local college sorority or fraternity. They often look for service projects.
- Contact a local church. They often look for ways to serve the community.
- Put an ad in your local newspaper. Many papers have a community calendar section where they will advertise your event and even advertise for volunteers as a free service.
- Contact your local high school. They might have a program for volunteering, or at least let you post a flyer on a bulletin board.

It is better to attract more volunteers than you really need because you will lose some along the way.

2.3 Conduct a volunteer orientation

Your volunteers should be enthusiastic, hardworking, willing to sacrifice their time, attract their friends to your organization, and remain dedicated to your organization even after the event. Where are you going to find good people like that? You're not. You will rarely find people like that. But you can motivate them to become that way. It all begins at your orientation.

The location of your meeting should attract people. Your conference room is a fine place to hold a meeting, I'm sure. But to generate more excitement, consider holding your meeting at a place where people would love to get a glimpse inside. Possible locations would include a celebrity's home, a luxurious estate, an exclusive country club, or an out-of-the-ordinary new building.

Those who should attend are chairpersons, committee members, staff, volunteers, and board members – everyone involved.

Your orientation may be the only time you can have a direct influence on your volunteers. *From the moment your volunteers step into your orientation until the time they leave, they are in YOUR realm of influence. What you do (or fail to do) during that time can make a difference in how willing your volunteers feel about helping you.*

The moment your volunteers arrive at your orientation, make them feel important. Greet them at the door. Record their contact information including telephone number, cell phone number, and email address. Give them a name tag. Have a small reception period. Provide a nice display of refreshments such as: pizza, sandwiches, a fruit platter or a vegetable tray with dip; perhaps some crackers and cheese, and a variety of drinks. Use people's names when talking with them. Introduce them to one another.

Then conduct the meeting. The object of the meeting is to get your volunteers to gain a desire to support your cause. Tell them about your organization; why it's so important to further its cause. Give examples of how it has helped people, the environment or the community. Have a guest speaker tell how the organization has helped him or her. If possible let the volunteers see first-hand what your organization does. Make an emotional appeal (1.18) like you would to guests at your fundraiser. Get everyone excited about being part of your event.

Invite each chairperson to give a short introduction so volunteers can catch the passion that drives the chairpersons to support the organization and the upcoming event. Give your potential volunteers the impression that you are well organized and have a plan. If you really are well organized and have a plan, all the better.

Volunteer Packets

Pass out volunteer packets. Volunteer packets should include:

- The agenda for the Volunteer Orientation (use an agenda at every meeting. Set precedence here)
- The printed program from last year (great sales tool for all to use)
- Event fact sheet (1.12)
- Dates of meetings coming up
- Phone numbers of chairpersons
- Donor slips (4.2)
- A list of incentives (1.15) that can be used to get people to donate, and when to use them

Orientation Agenda

- Everyone signs a sheet with contact information.
- The Event Chairperson welcomes everyone and makes the emotional appeal.
- Go through the volunteer packet.
- Each Chairperson explains the jobs they need to fill.
- Assign volunteers to chairpersons.
- Announce future training sessions.
- The Procurement Chair divides everyone into procurement teams.
  - Incentives are announced
  - Procurement ideas (4.4) are discussed
  - Team captains are chosen
  - Time and place for next procurement party is decided
- Show how to use the donor slips – everyone gets donor slips.
- Take pictures to go in the Scrapbook (15.1).

Use Last Year's Printed Program as a Sales Tool

Give everyone a printed program from the last event. Tell everyone that when asking for donations (whether it be in-kind Services, underwriting, auction items, etc.), don't forget to take this printed program with you. Use it as a sales tool. Show potential donors how donors' names were displayed in the printed program last year. It will help potential donors to visualize how their name will look.

It would also be helpful to show potential donors pictures of banners, signage, and other methods that were used to recognize the generosity of donors at the last event. Show them pictures of the audience to give an indication of how many people could be reading or hearing their names.

Tell Everyone to Bring a List of Friends

Tell everyone to bring a list of 10 people they know well, and their addresses. These people will get sent an invitation. But before the invitations go out, they will be given back to the originator for them to write a short personal note on each one. When the invitations are personalized, it means so much more and will have a more positive reaction.

Send a thank-you note to everyone who attended your meeting.

2.4   Get badges to identify volunteers

All committee members and volunteers at your event should be identified with a name badge or a ribbon or something to set them off and give them recognition as a helper. It is one of the many things you will do to make them feel important. It will also help guests identify a member of your staff in case they have a question. Name badges will also give your staff credibility in case they have to instruct guests to stand away from the silent auction tables that just closed, or invite guests to start migrating toward the dinner tables.

2.5   Care and feeding of volunteers

Prepare a handout for everyone helping at the event. It should include answers to all common questions such as:

- What time should we arrive?
- Where should we park?
- Is parking free?
- Where should we report?
- Who should we report to?
- Where can we leave our personal belongings? Consider using the coat-check as a place to store personal items, as there will always be someone there to watch them. Don't leave personal items unattended – not even for a minute.
- What are we supposed to wear?
- Do we get a bid number? Make sure all volunteers get a bid number. Volunteers make good bidders.
- Can we bring a guest with us?
- Are we going to eat? Provide food and drinks for the volunteers and a place for them to eat and relax when they are not busy working.
- When can we leave?

2.6   Keep track of volunteers

Maintain contact information including names, addresses, phone numbers, and email addresses of all staff, chairpersons, and volunteers. This list will also be used for sending thank-you letters (14.1) and asking for their help at the next event.

3. Underwriters Chair

As Underwriter Chair, it is your job to find people or organizations that will provide in-kind services, underwrite expenses, make cash contributions, or become sponsors. In other words, find ways to reduce your expenses.

Remember that when you ask someone to give you something, you need to be prepared to give something in return. Refer to Decide on Donor Incentives (1.15) for ideas.

Many large corporations have departments with names like "Community Development" that have budgeted money to help with fundraising in their community. Call around. Contact small and medium sized business as well. There are business owners in your community right now who have given thought to helping a non-profit organization. Make some calls. Find those people.

3.1 In-kind services

Make a list of all the things for which you will need money and how much it will cost. For example, you will need food, decorations, centerpieces, printing, entertainment, gifts, etc. See Establish the Budget (1.2) for possible expenses. Go to the people who provide the services you need and say:

"Will you donate your service 100%?"
If they say no, ask,
"Will you give it to us at half?"
"No".
"Will you give it to us at your cost?"
"No".
"Will you give it to us at cost plus 10%"?"
At some point in time they are going to agree.
Remember, if you don't ask, you won't get it.

Remember that people who provide services for free might need a lot of advance notice, perhaps 6 months. Then they are more able to work you in between their regular business.

3.2 Find underwriters

Make a list of all the expenses you expect to incur. Ask people to donate toward a particular expense. People who provide underwriting usually take care of all or part of a specific expense. Here are some possible items to have underwritten:

- Venue rental
- Advertising
- Food and catering
- Centerpieces
- Party favors
- Audio/visual
- Lighting equipment
- Entertainment
- Auctioneer
- Drinks
- Valet services
- Decorations
- Printing
- Postage
- Photography
- Newsletter

Ask people to underwrite the items on the list you created for in-kind-services that you couldn't get donated. People can underwrite the entire cost of the service or product, or make up what the provider of the service or product will not donate.

Before you ask people who you don't know to underwrite an expense, go back to people who underwrote something last year and ask them if they would do it again. Then visit the people who you asked to donate last year, but refused for whatever reason. Each year they are asked, they become a little more likely to donate. Let them know how badly they were missed and how badly their help is needed.

Make sure underwriters get recognized and thanked. In the printed program, publish the names of everyone who underwrote anything and what they underwrote. For example, "So-and-so's donation paid for this printed program" or "Mr. and Mrs. Donor underwrote the cocktail party". Your newsletter could also be used to thank your underwriters. Remember to send personalized thank-you notes to all underwriters.

3.3   Find cash contributors

This is for the dentist, the doctor, the lawyer, the architect, or anyone who cannot or will not donate a service or item. Approach the professional community and say:

"We are having this event and we're asking everyone in the professional community to donate $250.00. We will put their names in the program as a cash contributor." If they say no, say, "How about $150?"
"No."
"How about $50.00?"
"No."
"How about $25.00?"

Go after a specific amount of money. Don't say, "Well, we'd like you to give as much as you can." That sounds too wishy-washy.

Publish the names of everyone who contributed cash under the heading "Cash Contributors" in your printed program.

3.4 Find sponsors

Sponsorships can be set at various amounts, or levels. One example would be to set sponsorship levels at $2,500, $1,000 and $500. Call the sponsorships: Gold-Level, Silver-Level and Bronze-Level respectively. Each level of sponsorship receives benefits unique to that level.

Each sponsor should receive a personal phone call from the Executive Director or Event Chairperson after the event, and a personal thank-you letter from a beneficiary of the donation if possible. Following are possible benefits you can assign to each level of sponsorship:

Gold Level $2,500
- Recognition in the printed program as a Gold-Level supporter
- Full-page ad in the printed program
- A banner displaying your name and logo at the event
- Your name announced at the event
- Sponsor will receive a framed "Official Sponsor of..." certificate
- Name and logo in the newsletter and in promotional advertising
- Four tickets to the event

Silver Level $1,000
- Recognition in the printed program as a Silver-Level supporter
- Half-page ad in the printed program
- Signage displaying your name and logo at the event
- Sponsor will receive a framed "Official Sponsor of..." certificate
- Two tickets to the event

Bronze Level $500
- Recognition in the printed program as a Bronze-Level supporter

- Sponsor will receive a framed "Official Sponsor of..." certificate
- Two tickets to the event

These sponsor levels are examples only. You may want to have more than three levels of sponsors or higher amounts for each level. Also keep in mind that all benefits are negotiable. If someone wants to donate an amount apart from one of the three levels, negotiate the benefits.

Find Someone to Sponsor the Entire Event

Make a list of all your expected expenses. Then go out and find one major bank or corporation to underwrite your whole event. You'll have to create a presentation that shows how the corporation would benefit by being your only underwriter. You'll have to give the donor something in return (1.15). You could even go so far as to name the event after the corporation. For example:

- Find A Cure Gala – Presented by So-and-So Corporation
- Joe's Bank Summer Bash – To Benefit St. Mary's School

You will need to present detailed plans for your event, so that the decision-makers will feel you are well organized and will make their corporation look good to all who hear about your event, and to all who attend your event.

Invite a celebrity or community leader to help give the presentation. They will lend credibility to your event. They could be a national spokesperson, a local or national celebrity, community leader, or someone who has benefited from your organization's service. Show how the corporation will get a return on their investment. Talk about the quality of the guests you expect to attend the event and how you will market the corporation to them. Show how the people you serve will benefit from the corporation's generosity. Use pictures and emotional appeal (1.18).

3.5 Motivate committee members

You and your volunteers stand to receive a lot of rejection as you go around asking for money. It is important to keep your own spirits high and keep your committee members motivated. See Motivate and Retain Volunteers (1.19) for some ideas that could save you the headache of losing your discouraged helpers.

3.6 Print sponsor banners

There are so many things that can fall through the cracks if you're not careful. Be sure that all promises made to sponsors are kept. If you promised that a banner with their company name and logo will fly prominently over your event, make sure it happens.

Consider taking the banner to the sponsor for review and approval before the event. The banner will look impressive up close, and the fact that you spent the time and effort to show it to your sponsor will help build your relationship. After all, fundraising is a business built on relationships. Also, if there is a printing error on the banner, it is better to catch it early.

3.7 Make sure contributors get recognition

When your underwriters and contributors receive their printed program, you can bet the first thing they'll do is look for their names. Make sure they are not disappointed. Inform the Printed Program Chair that you want to review the program before it goes to press to make sure there is no contributor left behind, and that all names are spelled correctly.

3.8 Keep track of contributors

Maintain contact information including names, addresses and phone numbers of those who contributed money and in-kind services. Keep track of how much they contributed and what benefits were promised them in return. This list will also be used for sending thank-you letters (14.1) and later for contacting contributors before the next event. If you did a good job, they will most likely contribute again.

Underwriters Chair

4. Procurement Chair

4.1 Set procurement deadline

Procurement is the process of acquiring items and services to sell at your live and silent auctions. Keep procurement open as long as you can. Find out when you have to go to press with the Printed Program (9.2) and make that your deadline. If items come in too late to get included in the printed program you have some options:

1. Put them in the silent auction.
2. Consider using an Addendum (12.2) for live auction items.
3. Save them for next year's event.

4.2 Obtain donor slips

Donor Slips, also called Auction Donation Forms, should be used when soliciting items or services to sell at your silent and live auctions. *Every board member, staff member, committee member and volunteer should carry Donor Slips with them everywhere they go.* So print plenty.

Donor Slips should be two-part carbonless forms. One part goes to the person making the donation. The other part will be returned to the Procurement Chairperson. One Donor Slip should be used for each donation.

There are almost as many different donor slips as there are fundraisers. The following generic Donor Slip can be used as a pattern when producing your own donor slips.

10th **Annual Benefit Auction**
Donation Form

Name of Your Organization   Saturday March 11, 20xx
1234 East Dover Street   Hilton Hotel
My City, CA 99999   789 Hill Street
whatever@myemail.com ● (888) 123-4567   My City, CA

Contact Person _____

Company/Donor Name (to appear in the printed program) _____

_____

Mailing Address _____

Phone _____   Cell Phone _____

Email _____   Fax _____

Item description (to appear in the printed program). If gift certificate, state restrictions,

expiration date and how to redeem. _____

_____

_____

_____

_____

_____

_____

_____

_____

Fair Market Value _____

___ Item received

___ Donor will deliver by (date) _____

___ Donor will mail by (date) _____

___ To be picked up on (date) _____ at (location) _____

Committee member name _____ Phone _____

Donor Signature _____

(*Name of Your Organization*) is a 501(c)(3) non-profit organization. Your donation is tax
deductible to the fullest extent of the law. Please consult your accountant for details.

4.3 Organize procurement teams

Your first procurement meeting will happen during the Volunteer Orientation (2.3). During that meeting you will:

- Divide volunteers into teams
- Announce team and individual incentives
- Discuss procurement ideas
- Coordinate solicitation contacts to some degree so that the same prospect isn't approached more than once
- Pick team captains
- Decide on a time and place for the next procurement party

People are generally more motivated to procure when they are in teams. The teams should choose creative names (like, the Go-Getters) and compete with each other.

It is necessary to hold periodic procurement parties. These are show-and-tell parties to give teams bragging opportunities concerning items and services they've procured. There should also be discussion about:

- Which merchants were contacted?
- What items and services were procured?
- What strategies (4.4) were used to procure them?
- What incentives (1.15) were used to motivate merchants to donate?

Awards

Give awards to winning teams. These are the incentives you announced in your Volunteer Orientation (2.3). Individual awards can also be given for going above and beyond the call of duty. Awards can be given for best achievement in different categories. Categories can include:

- Highest number of items procured (items that can be counted should have a predetermined minimum value).
- Highest dollar value of combined team items and services.
- Most dollars raised at the auction.

Awards can be silly like a gold painted rock (the Gold Nugget Award) given to each member of a winning team. Or they can be more serious like dinner certificates or movie passes. Use your imagination to come up with some fun incentives and prizes.

Team Captains

Team captains should be outgoing and competitive. They should be dedicated to procuring quality items and services for the silent and live auctions. They should stay in touch with their team members on a regular basis and have their own team parties.

4.4   Procure items for silent and live auctions

Everyone should help procure items: board members, staff, committee members and volunteers.

Keep in mind that when you ask someone to donate something, you need to be prepared to give something in return. Be sure to read the task called Decide on Donor Incentives (1.15) for things you can do to give potential donors an incentive to donate. Also keep in mind that the most effective way to procure items is face-to-face contact with people. Donors have a harder time turning down people face-to-face than they do by mail, email, or over the phone.

When filling out the donor slips, make sure the Item Description is very detailed. The more potential buyers know about an item or service, the better the chance they will want it. At least they can't use the excuse that they didn't have enough information.

Get Former Donors to Donate Again.

Take donor slips to people who donated items for the last event and ask them to donate again. If you can get the same person who procured the item last time to approach the donor (with whom they have formed a relationship), that would be most effective.

Make your contacts as early as possible. Fill out the donor slip in advance so all you need is a signature, saving you and the donor time.

By the time you approach past donors for repeat donations, they should have received a thank-you note (14.1) and a Post-event Newsletter (5.2) from the prior event, which may make the donors more likely to donate again.

Always keep in touch with your donors. Do business with them. Send business to them. *The most successful fundraisers are those produced by organizations that have formed lasting relationships with potential donors, prospective guests, staff and volunteers.*

Double the Donation with One Question

Ask all of your procurement people to try an experiment. After a donor has agreed to donate an item or a service, ask this question: "This is going to be such a popular auction item. Could you possibly donate two?" This works particularly well when asking for items that didn't require the donor to buy at wholesale, such as:

- Rounds of golf
- Tickets to plays, movies, concerts, sport events, special events, etc.
- Ski passes
- Passes to zoos and theme parks
- Club memberships

Item Ideas

Question: What sort of items sell well at auctions?

Answer: Anything that two or more people in your audience will have an interest in buying. Ask yourself what type of guests will be attending? What are their interests? Are they sports fans? Travelers? Parents with children? Health nuts? Procure items you think they would like to have. Look at past events and notice which items sold well and which didn't. Try to get items that appeal to the majority of guests that will be attending your auction. Sell them what they want. Following are some ideas:

Items and Services Commonly Used

Procure items that people would buy anyway. If they buy them at your event they know their money is going to a good cause:

- Dinner for two
- A pair of movie, ballet, symphony, opera, sport event, concert or theatre tickets
- Vacation packages
- Car service or maintenance
- Flowers every month for a year
- Ski passes
- Massages, hair and beauty treatments
- Lawn care, landscaping, top soil, sprinkler installation
- Carpet cleaning
- Window washing
- Children's books and movies
- Gym and athletic club memberships
- What are the current fads? What are people clamoring to buy? Get that.
- A set number of hours of labor performed by a carpenter, an electrician, a plumber, a painter, a roofer, a cement layer, etc. (Suggest to your

tradesman that most likely the project they will be working on will take more time than the set number of hours – so they can bill for the rest of the time and make money. They may also be asked to return to bid on other projects, as well as be recommended to friends and neighbors.) Choose tradesmen that are competent, honest and safe, and make them appear that way in the description.

Items One Cannot Get Anywhere Else

These are things that you cannot get anywhere else but here at your auction. They would include:

- Something autographed by a celebrity
- A happy birthday wish lit up on a huge electric public billboard
- Be a guest conductor of an orchestra or symphony
- 18 holes of golf with a famous golfer or celebrity
- An American Flag flown over the U.S. Capitol. A flag can be obtained by writing to your U.S. Senator or Congressman.
- Concert tickets and a back-stage pass
- A reserved parking spot for one year
- Front row seats to a concert, game, graduation or play
- Movie, play, or TV walk-on role
- Lunch with a movie or TV cast
- A gourmet meal prepared at the winning bidder's home by a local chef
- Tickets to TV shows like Letterman, Leno, Oprah, and Saturday Night Live or the taping of a sitcom
- TV or radio station tour by a news anchor
- Principal for a day – parents buy this for one of their children
- A private performance or concert by a famous musician or entertainer

- A date with a bachelor or bachelorette – include a date package
- Tickets to a popular concert in a distant city, round trip airfare for 2, and a night at a nice hotel.
- Autographed basketball by an NBA team.
- A kiss from a model or celebrity
- Shadow a government official or famous person for a half day. Lunch or dinner included
- Go around with a TV news crew
- A private after-hours shopping spree
- A caricature drawn by a famous cartoonist
- A private anything tour – zoo, castle, expensive home
- A speaking role on air at a radio station

Speaking of kisses, I am aware of two women whose kisses I sold, who eventually married the men who bought their kisses. It was their first introduction to each other. You never know how an auction might change the course of someone's life.

More Fun with Celebrities

Here are some opportunities revolving around someone with celebrity status. A celebrity could be a TV or movie star, a popular entertainer, a local radio or TV personality, a government official, a CEO of a corporation, or a local or national popular sports figure. Consider the following:

- Lunch or dinner with a celebrity
- Have a celebrity recognize you at a restaurant and join you and your party for lunch
- Be escorted to an event by a celebrity
- An hour of one-on-one training with a famous sports person
- A celebrity to record a greeting on your voice mail or answering machine

- A celebrity to mow your grass. Throw a lawn mower into the package.
- A photo with a celebrity. After you sell this opportunity to the highest bidder, announce that anyone who matches the bid will get their photo with the celebrity as well.
- A back-stage pass to meet the celebrity after a performance.
- Once I sold a lunch with the cast of a TV show. When I sold it, the cast, which were sitting at a table together, all got up, went over to the winning bidder and congratulated her. The photographer took a picture of her with the cast, and sent it to her later. It was a very nice way to make the winning bidder feel good, and have good memories.

Jewelry and Clothing

Necklaces, bracelets and earrings make fine auction items. But keep in mind that rings, which require an exact fit on someone's finger, will normally not attract much attention unless it can be exchanged for one that fits perfectly. Ask merchants who donate clothing to allow the buyer to come to the store and exchange the clothing for a more suitable size.

All jewelry and clothing should be modeled (12.9), and the modeling should start when guests begin to arrive. The model approaches a guest and says, "This matching bracelet and necklace will be on the live auction tonight. Would you be interested in taking a closer look?" Then she can take it off and let the guest try it on if they would like. People generally do not like to buy jewelry or clothing that they have not had a chance to touch and see up close or try on. Consider having a hand-held mirror available.

Jewelry should never be displayed on a table for security reasons. Jewelry displayed on a table makes a tempting prize for a thief. Jewelry should always be worn by a model.

Mystery Box

Fill a nicely decorated box with a bunch of great items; something you know most anybody would like. Announce the approximate retail value. Then sell this mystery box without divulging what is inside.

Vase Filled with Money

Sell a vase. Start the bidding at $5.00 and go up in increments of $5.00. When the Auctioneer reaches 25 or 30 dollars, he or she pauses and says, "You know, ladies and gentlemen, this vase would be much more interesting with something in it. Hey, I have an idea. Everyone reach into your pocket and pull out a one-dollar bill. Let's fill this vase with money. Everyone pull out a one-dollar bill. If you need change, we will make it for you. If you need a loan, we'll give you one. Hold your dollar in the air until one of our volunteers comes to get it."

The key to making this work is the have enough volunteers to gather all the money in one minute or less. The money is put into the vase and the Auctioneer says, "Doesn't that vase look more interesting now? Who'll give me thirty five dollars?" Many hands will go up and the Auctioneer pauses for fun. "Anybody?" This is where the Auctioneer can show off his or her bid-calling by going through the numbers at warp speed, "35 now 40 now 45 now 50 now 55 now 60 now 65..." until the last hand is up. This can be a lot of fun.

Bundled Items

Items can be sold at auction separately, or in a bundle. If you have many small items, you may want to bundle them. Put them in a pretty basket or other decorative container. I worked with a Procurement Chair that asked everybody – staff, committee chairs, volunteers, and board members (and all their friends) – to bring a bottle of wine. All the bottles were put into a donated wheelbarrow and auctioned off.

You could ask everyone to bring a particular tool, and fill a tool chest. Have everyone bring a CD or DVD. What if you had a Hollywood theme? In your invitation you could ask everyone to bring a DVD to the event with them. Collect all the DVDs in a basket and sell the basket.

Increase Value by Framing Items

All paintings, prints, posters, flags, autographed pictures, certificates of authenticity, etc. should be framed. Sports memorabilia such as an autographed jersey should be framed – not thrown in a bag or hung on a hanger. Anything that a person would buy to display in his or her home or office should be framed, ready to hang on the wall. Autographed basketballs, footballs, and baseballs should be encased in plastic or put on a small stand of some kind. Framed items display more nicely than unframed items and sell for considerably more. The way an item is presented can make a big difference in how much it sells for.

Include Airfare with Destinations

A condo on the beach might make a fine auction item, but a condo on the beach with airfare included makes a fabulous auction item. You'll generate more interest if you provide a way to get to far away destinations. Many airlines are generous with ticket donations but might require you to use only their tickets at the exclusion of other airline tickets.

Swap Items with Out-of-state Organizations

If you procure a weekend stay at a nice hotel in your city, instead of trying to sell it at your auction to a local guest, contact some organizations in popular tourist cities and ask to swap hotels. People would rather stay in a hotel outside of their home town. If you can find an organization in another location that might have or will soon procure a local hotel stay for their upcoming auction, see if you can make a trade. It would be a win/win for both organizations. Think of other items you could swap, such as tickets to a concert or sporting event, ski passes, theatre tickets, or a week-long stay in a condo. A continued relationship with other organizations could lead to some sweet deals.

Used Car

Ask a dealer to donate a used car, and see if you can procure the following items and services for the car:

- Tune-up
- Oil change
- Body work and new paint
- New tires
- New windshield wipers
- Interior cleaning

Use the incentives discussed in Decide on Donor Incentives (1.15) to entice your potential donors. When all the work is complete, you have a pretty nice used car for someone to buy for their 16-year-old child or grandchild. And all the money is profit.

Auctioning Puppies

I've sold a lot of puppies. If you are going to sell a puppy, consider the following:

- It should be at least eight weeks old. Nine is better.
- It should be a purebred and properly papered.
- It should have had its first exam and shots.
- Popular breeds have more general appeal.
- The puppy should be accompanied by a professional handler throughout the entire event.
- Do not let the winning bidder take delivery of the puppy on the day of the event. Rather, deliver the

puppy to the new owners two or three days later. That will allow the new owners time to get their home prepared for the new arrival.

- Reserve the right to not sell the puppy. This is in case you feel the winning bidder will not take good care of it for whatever reason.

You should know that auctioning puppies (and other pets) are a topic of concern with animal rights groups. Before you decide to auction a puppy, please read what The Humane Society of the United States and the American Kennel Club (AKC) have to say about it. Go to **www.LetsDoAnAuction.com/resources.htm**.

Specialty Auctions

A specialty auction is one that caters to people with particular interests. The benefit of having a specialty auction is that you can advertise and market to a target audience. Here are some possible categories of specialty items:

- Art
- Wine
- Sporting equipment in general
- Sporting equipment specific
  - o Ski equipment
  - o Hiking and camping equipment
  - o Fishing gear
  - o Etc.
- Wedding items and services
- Home improvement items and services
- Baby stuff
- Toys
- Furniture
- Chef – auction off the services of local chefs
- Electronics
- Bachelors and Bachelorettes with dating packages

Ask Your Guests for Ideas

Why not mail a questionnaire and a return envelope to past guests, especially past bidders, and invite them to list three items they'd like to see in your auction? The ideal situation is to have items in the auction that people want. What better way to find out what they want than to ask them. And if they know that you are going to try to procure an item that they are planning to buy, they might decide to wait until your auction to buy it.

To make the invitation even more personal, ask your biggest bidders from last year to coffee or breakfast or lunch and say, "You've been so generous to us year after year, what are the items you'd like to see in the auction?" Do you think they'd be flattered? They may say, "Well, my wife and I have been thinking of a cruise to Alaska." Then you go get a cruise to Alaska. You don't want guests leaving your auction saying, "Gosh, there just wasn't anything here I wanted to buy."

When you've procured an item requested by someone, call that person to tell them you've procured it. Invite them to the Pre-auction Open House (4.10).

Some Items Don't Sell Well

Once I was given the task of selling a bridge. It was a beautiful sturdy 9-foot bridge made with steel and redwood, made to go over a small creek, pond or rock garden in someone's backyard, worth about $2,500. The problem was, few guests, if any, had a creek, pond, or rock garden in their backyard, let alone, one over which they needed a bridge.

I started the bidding at $1,000, hoping to get a bite. I thought if only one person was interested, it would be better to start a little higher than I normally would. No one bid. I dropped the opening bid to 900, then to 800, 700, 600, and then to 500. At $500 a man raised his hand, and guess what? He was the only bidder and bought the bridge for $500.

What do we learn from this? Unless you want to sell items at bargain prices, procure items that you think two or more people will want. By the way, the bridge was donated, so $500 was raised from the sale which wouldn't have been raised otherwise. Just keep in mind: it takes at least two interested buyers to have an auction.

Be Able to Answer Two Questions

Before you go after auction items, be able to answer two questions:

1. How much money do you want to raise? (1.2)
2. What is the money going for? (1.1)

Answer these questions with enthusiasm when asked by potential donors. Potential donors need a compelling reason and a specific amount that they can picture in their minds in order to catch your vision. (See Catch the Vision (1.1) for more explanation.) When they catch your vision, they tend to get involved, and even cheer you on. When that happens another interesting thing takes place. You and all your helpers get inspired to work harder.

Where to Get Items

There are at least eight potential resources from which you can procure auction items:

1. Get former donors to donate again.
2. You, committee members and volunteers – what item or service can YOU provide. What item, hobby or skill do you have that can be auctioned off?
3. Spouse or significant other. Can they teach a skill; provide a service?
4. Friends and family – people who really like you – You may have heard the saying that every person on earth is separated from every other person by only **six**

degrees. That means that your friend's sister's boss has a cousin whose best friend could get you that outrageous auction item you want. I call it **Six Degrees of Procurement**. It's all about networking and forming relationships. AND it's all about asking. You could possibly be only a few networking steps away from someone who could help you procure just about anything.

5. Neighbors and co-workers – people who know you're a good person

6. Merchants where you shop. You bring them business. Ask them to donate. If your committee members, staff, board of directors, and volunteers carry Donor Slips (4.2) everywhere they go, they can ask for donations where ever they spend money. If they go to a restaurant, they should ask to talk with the owner or manager after desert. Every shopping trip should include a talk with the store's owner. Every gym bag should contain donor slips. Anywhere they go for entertainment, they should ask for a donation.

7. Vendors and suppliers to your business. They love you. You give them money. Ask them for a donation for a good cause. The painter, the sprinkling system installer, the roofer, the electrician, the man who delivers water, your CPA, your attorney, the gym where you exercise, are all potential donors.

8. Cold calls (see below).

Cold-Call Strategies

Here are some guidelines regarding making cold calls:

- Don't go alone on cold calls. Go in a group of three or four. You will be less nervous, less likely to wait, you'll motivate each other, brainstorm among yourselves, and you'll flatter the potential donors.

- Ask for something specific. Instead of saying, "What can you give us?", say, "Can you donate the plasma TV?"
- Potential donors are interested in the quality as well as the quantity of the people attending your auction. Know the power of the guests that will come to your event, the area in which they live, what they do, if they're presidents, vice presidents, average age, etc. People who give to auctions want to know how it can be good marketing for them.
- Contact everyone around a merchant who donated and let the potential donor know that his or her neighbor donated.
- Contact donors' competitors to let them know their competition will be featured at your event and ask them to donate too.
- Face to face contact is best.
- Strike up a conversation with people next to you at the bus stop, the train, in the checkout line, on a plane. Find out what they do. They'll eventually ask you what YOU do. Always keep a handful of your business cards with you and a pen to write down phone numbers etc. You might create some lasting friendships along the way.
- Every board member, staff member, chairperson, committee member and volunteer should carry donor slips everywhere they go. Did I mention that?
- Don't hesitate to ask for donations from people who refused to donate last year. Every year that they get asked to donate, the chances of them donating get better. Why do you suppose commercials are played over and over again? Because each time someone sees or hears that commercial, they get closer to making that purchase. Don't give up too soon.
- Be a mentor. Many people find it intimidating to ask someone for a donation. Often, procurement teams just need a little push to get started. So make an

appointment to join a team to go around and ask business owners for donations. All the team needs are a few successful experiences to get them fired up.

Look What Can Happen

Consider the procurement possibilities. Let's say you have only 16 volunteers to procure items. That includes staff, board members, and volunteers; everyone involved. They are divided into four teams with four people on each team. Watch what could happen:

- **Former donors** are contacted and 10 items are procured.
- Each **volunteer** donates an item or service for a total of 16.
- Each **spouse or significant** other comes up with a donation, for a total of 16.
- One **friend** and one **family member** make a donation for a total of 32.
- One **neighbor** and one **co-worker** make a donation for a total of 32.
- One **merchant**, where volunteers shop, makes a donation for a total of 16.
- One **Vendor/Supplier** makes a donation for a total of 16.
- Four successful **cold calls** per team generate 16 donations.

That's a total of 154 items or services that can be sold at the silent or live auction.

4.5 Artwork considerations

Why do people buy art? I've discovered the following reasons:

- It goes well with the couch
- To decorate a home or office
- They collect the artist's work
- It will make a good investment
- It makes them feel good – they bond with it
- It reminds them of something
- It adds a sense of culture to their life
- To show it off
- They just plain like it – art is an emotion thing
- To give to someone as a gift

So it only makes sense to display and describe the artwork in a way that makes it easy for potential buyers to become attached to it. Display artwork like it is displayed in an art gallery. Visit an art gallery and see what they do to make artwork appealing. Consider the following:

- All pictures should be framed. Even prints.
- All pictures should be displayed on an easel.
- Get an appraisal if possible. When the Item Describer says, "This painting (sculpture, antique piece, etc.) was appraised last month by Fredrick's Appraising for $5,650 and comes with a certificate attesting to that," it lends credibility and value to the artwork.
- The printed program should contain a detailed description of the art work and the artist and places where the artist's work has been on display. The same description should accompany the actual artwork and be described by the Item Describer (12.14).
- If logistically possible, consider shining a spotlight on the artwork from above like they do in a gallery. Note that a spotlight shined on a painting from the *side* might cause annoying glare.
- Get the artist to explain his or her inspiration for creating the artwork. Also, announce that the winning bidder will have an opportunity to meet and talk with the artist.

- For well know artists, there is a feeling that a low purchase price could decrease the value of other artwork by that artist. So consider a minimum bid.
- For emerging artists, the auction offers good visibility for the artist. Consider any reasonable bid.

4.6 Services that can be sold

I've divided services into three areas: Common Services, Teaching a Skill, and Providing an Experience. For some services, you'll need to set a limit to the number of hours the service will be performed. See what you think.

Common Services

Babysitting
Yard work
Lawn mowing
Snow shoveling
Landscape design
Baking
Cooking a meal
Cookies delivered every week for a month
Fresh bread delivered every week for month
Hosting a picnic
Catering
Washing windows
Front row seats at an event
A VIP reserved parking spot
Celebrity to show up at a birthday or company party
Photo with a celebrity
Family/personal portrait
Host a birthday party
Tutoring
Provide musical talent at an event
Painting – house external or internal
Face painting at a birthday party

Interior design
House cleaning and/or organizing
Once-a-month dog wash and grooming
Pet sitting
Dog walking
Dog training
Makeup make-over
Haircut, color
Manicure, pedicure
Car wash
Financial consulting
Tax preparation
Will preparation
Computer repair
Computer consulting e.g. setting up a home wireless
       network
Dental work
Grocery shopping for someone
Transporting people to places – taxi service
Limo service
Heating/Air conditioning services
Shoe shining
Shopping consulting
Car repair/maintenance
Massage therapy
Fitness training
Deliver a meal/desert
Deliver a week's worth of meals/deserts
Sewing
Quilting
Use of a vacation home
Use of a motor home
Tickets to the zoo
Carpentry work
Electrical work
Plumbing work
Housecleaning
Handyman – rent-a-husband

Hot tub party
Pool maintenance
Roof repair
Continuing education classes
Stringing Christmas lights on your house – and taking
them down

Teaching a skill

Fly fishing
Skiing
Golfing
Tennis
Weight lifting
Surfing
Self-defense
Scrap-booking
Flower arranging
Cooking
Canning
Baking
Sewing
Quilting
Dancing
Musical instrument
Singing lessons
Drawing/Art lessons
First aid training
Survival training
Dutch oven cooking
Cake decorating
Secrets to good photography

Providing an experience

Fishing trip – fly fishing, deep-sea fishing, etc.
Snowmobiling
Cross country skiing

98

Snowshoeing
Hunting
Target shooting
Rollerblading
Ice skating
Rock climbing
Motorcycle riding
Waterskiing
Skydiving
Scuba diving
Snorkeling
Horseback riding
Camping
River running
Canoeing
Kayaking
Sailing
Cross country bicycling
Kiss from a celebrity
A date with someone
Airplane ride
Lunch, tennis or golf with a movie star, TV/radio
    personality, politician, contest winner or other
    celebrity
One hour of one-on-one training from a well-known
    athlete (college, high school, or professional)
Four-wheeling on the back roads
Be a guest conductor of an orchestra or a symphony
Be a radio co-disc jockey
A guided tour of a TV studio by a news anchor
    person
Parasailing

4.7   Decide on number of live auction items

One of the questions I'm often asked is, "How many items should be in the live auction?" Consider these two facts:

1. The more items you have, the more money you're going to make.
2. The longer you take, the more people are going to leave.

It's been my experience that after an hour, people tend to get restless and some start to leave. However, on the other hand, the more items you have, the more money you are going to raise. On the other hand, if you have items that the majority of guests will want to bid on, then they'll stay longer. But since the recommended goals are to raise a lot of money AND send people home happy, then it would make sense to end sooner than later. Some would suggest keeping the length of the live auction to an hour or less. Others would say an hour-and-a-half or two hours is okay. Are you getting the feeling there's not an absolute answer to this question?

With that in mind, let's decide how many items we can sell within an hour. An item can usually be sold in 3 to 4 minutes. That includes the time it takes to describe the item and sell it to indecisive bidders. If you feel your items will average 4 minutes a piece, then 15 items is your limit (4 minutes per item x 15 items = 60 minutes total).

If you think your items fit into the 3-minute-per-item category, then plan on no more than 20 items an hour (3 x 20 = 60). Two minutes per item will sell 30 items in an hour.

I'll tell you what makes bidding on an item go over the 3 to 4 minute limit. Bidding will take longer when two parties are bidding against each other toward the end of the bidding, and each party has to discuss with their significant other how badly they really want the item and how they are going to afford it. A skilled Auctioneer will get people thinking and bidding faster. An unskilled Auctioneer can draw out an auction for what will seem like forever.

Look in the Post-event Evaluation (1.20) that was developed from the last event. How many items were sold at the live auction? Were there any comments about the number of items being too high or too low? If you still can't decide how many items to put in the live auction, go with 15 to 20 and see how that works. Make sure to put remarks in YOUR Post-event Evaluation.

4.8   Assign items to silent and live auctions

It is possible for a good Auctioneer to sell almost any silent auction item for more than that item will fetch in the silent auction. I've been given items from the silent auction that didn't get a single bid, and sold them in the live auction at near retail value. When **The Four Objectives of a Successful Fundraiser** have been achieved, people get caught up in the thrill of bidding, and what were once non-selling silent auction items, become hot items in the live auction. So here are some guidelines to consider when dividing items between silent and live auctions:

- Live auction items should be among the more expensive items.
- Live auction items should be items that will need an explanation in order to generate interest.
- Sprinkle the live auction with less expensive, popular items so everyone can have fun bidding; not just those with lots of money.

4.9   Arrange for receiving and storing items

You will need an area in which to receive and store auction items before the event. You may also need to arrange to pick up items from donors.

In the case that an item is difficult to transport because of its size, the donor might suggest that he or she deliver the item directly to the event on the day of the event. This may seem like a good idea at the time, but beware. You are taking a risk that something may prevent the delivery of that item. I've been to events where an item just never showed up in time for the auction.

The donor may simply forget, or not have the resources to make the delivery, or even decide not to make the donation at the last minute. You might also be required to take delivery of the item at the event at a time when it is inconvenient for you. So, just be aware of the risks. Call the donor a day or two prior to the event to give a reminder. Have a plan ready to use in case the item cannot be delivered by the donor.

I've always thought that it is better to be in control of all your items rather than be at the mercy of someone else.

The Live Auction Chair is in charge of delivery of large auction items to winning bidders. That means if you sell a large item with the intent of delivering it the next day, you will need somewhere to store it over night. Do you have a place? What if after selling a large item at the auction, the buyer cannot take delivery for a few days? In that case, you're going to need a place to store that item for a few days. Coordinate post-event item storage needs with the Auction Chair (12.7).

4.10 Hold a pre-auction open house

People have a hard time buying expensive items that they have not had a chance to inspect, talk over with their spouses, and think about how to afford. In an effort to remove all excuses for not bidding on an item, hold a Pre-auction Open House about a week before the event.

Send invitations to everyone who has purchased tickets. In the invitation, list all of your big-ticket items. List your artwork and your jewelry. List anything that you feel people need to inspect before buying. Invite everyone to come and enjoy refreshments, meet some of the organization's key people, and have a look at the expensive items that will be sold at the auction. Keep the Open House going all day to accommodate everyone's schedule. Treat guests like royalty when they arrive.

Go ahead and display the less expensive items if you have them, but the purpose of the Open House is to give a preview of your expensive items. You'll know that everyone who comes will have an interest in buying, and when you prepare a seating chart (8.3), you can seat them closer to the front than the back.

Can't Hold an Open House?

If you can't hold an Open House, send a brochure describing the major items in detail with pictures. You can also send a postcard inviting your guests to view the major auction items on your website. Many people just won't make major purchases without having some time to think about it.

4.11 Deliver auction items to the event

Auction items will have to be delivered to the location of the event and set up before the guests arrive. Make sure you allow plenty of time to make that happen. Also plan to provide adequate transportation such as trucks to haul the items. You may also want to plan on providing tables and table cloths on which to display the items.

Don't wait until the last minute to find a truck or people to carry heavy items. Coordinate with the Volunteer Chair.

4.12   Determine minimum bids

When Not to Use Minimum Bids

There is an advantage to not using predetermined minimum bids. I usually start the bidding of an item at 1/4 to 1/3 of its estimated retail value. But if I feel the item won't draw much interest, I'll start high, say, half of the retail value. Then if only one person bids, we make half of retail instead of one third of retail.

If I think an item will draw a lot of bids, I might start at 1/10th of retail value to get everyone raising their hands. That's a good way to get a lot of people to experience the thrill of bidding, which is fun for everyone, and usually results in a high bid in the end. I can only adjust the starting bid if there is not a predetermined minimum bid.

When to Use Minimum Bids

There is one advantage of using predetermined minimum starting bids, and that is to reduce bidding time. Let's say I'm selling an autographed basketball and start the bidding at $300. No bids. I go down to $250, then $200, then $100, then $50. Finally, a hand goes up and I begin selling.

The next item to be auctioned is 18 holes of golf and dinner for four people. I start the bidding at $250. Now the audience has been conditioned. They know if nobody bids, I'll take the starting bid way down. So they will wait to bid until I drop the starting bid to a low number.

If there is a predetermined starting bid for each item, and it is printed in the program, I'm obligated to start the bidding at that price.

What if no one bids at the starting bid? In that case I say, "All right then, let's move on to the next item." Then at some point during the auction or at the end of the auction, I say, "Ladies and gentlemen, I've just been given authorization to start the bidding on this item below the minimum bid printed in your program."

Consignment Items

Consignment items are those items that you sell and give the wholesale cost back to the donor. For instance, say you want to sell a piano that you obtained from a piano dealer on a consignment of $3,000. After you sell the piano you must pay the piano dealer $3,000. Anything over $3,000 you get to keep.

What if you only get $3,000 for the piano? Then you don't make anything. That's why on consignments I always start the bidding above the consignment value. That way if there is only one bidder, you'll make *something*. In the case of the piano, I would let the audience know that we have a minimum bid of $3,100. If no one bids, then the piano simply is returned to the piano dealer. If the piano sells, then it is delivered to the buyer and we rejoice in our profit.

I prefer to use minimum starting bids on all consignment items rather than starting below the consignment amount and hope bidders will bid over the consignment amount. I hate telling the audience, after the bidding has started, that there was an undisclosed minimum amount I needed to get and that it had not been reached. I think when I do that, the bidders feel I have wasted their time, and wonder how many more items have an undisclosed minimum bid. When I get the audience caught up in the thrill of bidding, I don't want to tell them that no one wins.

Set the minimum bid a little higher than the consignor's portion. Then if you only get one bid, you make a little money rather than just break even.

I don't think it matters whether or not you publish the minimum bid with the item description in the printed program. But the minimum bid should be announced when the item is described, either by the Item Describer (12.14) or the Auctioneer. If no one bids, then go on to the next item. It's better to return an item to a consignor rather than lose money.

4.13 Keep track of donors

Maintain contact information including names, addresses and phone numbers of those who donate items or services to be put in the silent or live auctions. This list will be used for sending thank-you letters (14.1).

4.14 Keep track of consignment items

Keep track of consignment items and make sure the donor gets the consignment amount or consignment item returned. By the way, keep all consignment items in pristine condition so you're not returning a scratch-&-dent item. I'm not a fan of consignment items but I have sold a lot of them.

5. Publicity/Public Relations Chair

5.1 Distribute news releases

A good way to increase visibility and awareness about your upcoming fundraiser is to get a newspaper or magazine (or both) to print an article about your event. A common way to make that happen is to send out news (or press) releases.

Newspapers and magazines are constantly looking for good material to print. The more they attract readers, the more they attract advertisers. The more advertising they sell, the more money they make. They rarely fill up all the space in their publications with news their reporters dig up. So they rely on unsolicited news releases to fill the gaps.

Out of the many unsolicited news releases received each day, a newspaper or magazine editor must decide which ones will appeal to readers, and out of those, which ones can be relied on to be truthful, so as not to mislead readers.

When confronted with material from an unfamiliar source, an editor must be skeptical. Your news release about your fundraiser will have a better chance of being printed if the editor has become familiar with the reputation of your organization. Therefore, it is important to cultivate a relation with an editor by periodically sending news releases about your organization before you send a news release about your up-coming fundraiser.

Call the newspaper or magazine and find out who the editor or associate editor is that deals with special events. Following are tips you should know, that will increase the chances of your news release getting published.

Tips on Writing a Good News Release

Remember who your target audience is. When you write a news release, your target audience is not potential donors or guests; your target audience is the *journalist* who reads your news release. Journalists look for interesting, newsworthy stories that are out-of-the-ordinary. A good news release is one that can be printed without a lot of revising. Write your story like you would see it in a newspaper or magazine.

Make sure your news is newsworthy. *Remember that the purpose of your news release is to inform, not to advertise.* A newsworthy story is one that the reader will find helpful, interesting, motivating, stimulating, or emotional. It should make the reader want to say, to his or her spouse, "Honey, listen to this..." It will illustrate that which makes your organization different. It will show why someone would want to come to YOUR fundraiser over another. If your story is compelling enough, a reporter might ask to do a feature article about your organization.

Use a descriptive headline. The headline is your first, and perhaps, only chance to capture the reader's attention and keep him or her reading. Rather than using a headline to announce your fundraiser, create a headline that demonstrates your fundraiser's newsworthiness. Look at your local newspaper for hundreds of examples of descriptive headlines.

Answer the five "W" questions in the first paragraph. They are: Who are you? What are you doing that's so great? Where is the event going to be? When is the event going to be held? Why are you holding the event? The heading and the first paragraph should cover the main points of your event. You grabbed the reader's attention in the headline. The first paragraph is where you hold the reader's attention. The first paragraph is like an "elevator speech". Imagine you are in an elevator with someone whose help you need. You only have 10 floors to tell your story. What are you going to say?

Identify a problem and show how you solve it. The rest of the news release will cover the details. Talk about your cause and how your organization makes your part of the world a better place. Give examples of what your organization has done to solve a problem. Explain what you plan to accomplish with the money you will raise at your event.

Analyze newspaper articles. Pick out some articles you like and ask yourself what makes them helpful, interesting, motivating, stimulating, or emotional. Then read them again. But this time look at how they are written. Notice how the title grabs your attention. See if all five "W" questions are answered. Observe how the details support the heading and opening paragraph. Identify a consistent pattern in the way articles are presented. Save and analyze all articles written about special events.

Include a photograph. It is a good idea to include photos. Photos make your news release more interesting as long as the photos relate directly to your story. Consider a photo from your last event, or a photo of the featured celebrity at your up-coming event. Photos should be 5 x 7 inches or larger, and good quality. Newspapers like black and white photos, but will accept color. Magazines like color photos. On the back of each photo, identify the people in the photo and what they are doing. The photos should capture the reader's attention and make him or her want to know more.

Consider these mechanics. Use letterhead so your organization is easily identified. Don't be wordy or use flowery language. If you can say the same thing in a shorter sentence, do it. Keep your sentences short. Your news release should be no longer than two pages in length, either double or single spaced. The font should be Times New Roman or Arial and the font size should be 12. Proof read and re-proof read your news release to catch grammatical errors and typos. Such errors may affect your credibility.

Formatting a News Release

There is no official standard way to format a news release. However, some publishers do require certain guidelines to be followed. Before you write a news release, contact the newspaper or magazine to which you are going to submit a news release, and ask about format requirements. Many formatting guidelines do include the following:

Always include the contact person's name, phone number, and email address within your organization so an editor can get in touch with that person. Also, type the words "FOR IMMEDIATE RELEASE" or "FOR RELEASE AFTER (and state the release date)" at the top of the news release. Start your first paragraph with the name of your city and state, followed by today's date.

At the top of page 2 repeat the title, contact name, phone number, email address and identify it as page 2. At the end of your news release, skip a line and center the following: "###", indicating the end of the news release. Consider the following example:

FOR IMMEDIATE RELEASE

Contact:
Mary Smith
Development Director
(999) 123-4567
msmith@myemail.com

Celebrities to Gather at Fundraising Gala

Surf City, CA, March 24, 20xx: Entertainers, radio and TV personalities, and government officials will make a rare appearance together at the XYZ Foundation's annual Spring Fundraising Gala on April 20, at the City Center

110

Hotel, 2715 Augusta Avenue in Surf City. The money raised will go to support and expand the after-school programs run by the Foundation. The Gala will have a Hollywood theme and include dinner, entertainment, silent and live auctions.

The rest of the news release explains about your organization, how it fills a need in the community, and how the money raised is going to be used. It can include statistics, quotes from key people, ticket prices and how to purchase them.

###

5.2 Newsletters

Newsletters serve to do the following:

- Help to keep the name of your organization on the minds of the potential donors and guests all year.
- Provide a place for vendors to advertise.
- Provide a place for contributors to be recognized.
- Provide a place to publicly praise and recognize good things that volunteers do.
- Tell people all about your upcoming event.

I suggest using at least four different mailers, two of them being newsletters:

1. After the last event you send out post-event newsletters (described below).

2. Then you send out Save-the-date Postcards (7.2).
3. Then you send out pre-event newsletters (described below).
4. Finally, you send out the Invitations (7.4).

If you do this, everyone on your mailing list will hear from you at least four times before your event.

Pre-event Newsletter

There should be an article in your pre-event newsletter advertising your event. The article should include:

- Date and time
- Location
- Theme (if there is one)
- Attire
- Ticket price
- Entertainment
- Celebrity attending
- How much you raised last year
- Where last years money went
- How much you intend to raise this year
- What the money is going to be used for
- Honorary Chairperson's name
- Chairpersons' names
- A sneak preview of auction items – If someone sees that an item they have been thinking of buying, they may postpone buying that item until your auction. That won't happen unless you let them know in advance.
- Corporate sponsors
- Underwriters
- Those providing in-kind services
- Pictures from the last event. People in the pictures should be identified by name.
- Recognition of anyone who did something amazing or is in charge of something. People love recognition.

Look for any excuses to recognize vendors, volunteers, donors, etc. Mention as many people, by name, as you can, and tell about their accomplishments, donations, time invested, etc. Include photos. Make sure everyone you recognize is on your mailing list.

- Those who purchased tables (7.5)
- Table Hosts (7.6)

The newsletter should go to the following people:

- Everyone on your mailing list (7.1)
- Board members
- The media
- All volunteers
- Donors

Tell vendors that their names are going to be in your newsletter and ask if they would like to put an advertisement in your newsletter, giving them double exposure. Of course they will have to pay for their advertisement, helping to offset your cost.

Try to get someone to underwrite your newsletter. Then, in the newsletter, in an obvious place it should say, "This newsletter is brought to you by *underwriter's name*." People love to receive recognition. Did I mention that?

Post-event Newsletter

It is important that the post-event newsletter be sent out. It is like broadcasting the final score of the big game. Everyone involved in the event will be interested in the outcome. The headline should say:

We Made it! $90,000 Raised

The post-event newsletter should go to everyone who received the pre-event newsletter, plus anyone else who was involved in the event. This newsletter should include a nice recap of the event with plenty of pictures and names.

5.3   Contact local press to do a feature article

One of the reasons you want the local press to do a feature article about your organization is to raise public awareness about what your organization does and what effect it has. Then, when people receive an invitation to your fundraiser, they will remember the article they saw, and might be more inclined to purchase a ticket.

What makes the feature article newsworthy is the story about the fundraiser you are conducting, the ambitious financial goal you have set, and all the wonderful things you have planned for the event. On a slow news day, the newspaper will run the article. You don't know when that slow news day will be, so contact newspapers, magazines, radio and TV early. Let them decide how soon before your event they should do an interview.

Provide a Community Service

A good public relations strategy is to have the people for whom your organization serves do a community project. Have them refurbish a playground, clean up a vacant lot, or paint over graffiti. Call someone in city government and ask for suggestions. Then make a call to the local newspaper and TV stations and tell them your intentions for possible media attention.

5.4   Get on all local community calendars

Contact local newspapers, magazines, radio and TV to get your fundraiser on their community calendars. It's just another way of getting your name in front of people. Community calendars are usually a public service and therefore a free way to advertise.

114

5.5   Invite the press to the event

Call local newspapers, magazines, radio and TV and invite the people who normally write about society events or report on community functions to join you at your event. Put them on your mailing list and send them everything you send to everyone else. You may get a post-event write-up in a newspaper or magazine. Your event might get mentioned during the evening news.

Be clear about expectations. TV people will usually only stay 30 minutes unless the station is underwriting the event, in which case they might stay longer. Newspaper and magazine people may stay for the entire event in which case you should offer complementary tickets to all your event functions. If you have a VIP reception before the general reception, invite the media to that. Otherwise invite them to the general reception for appetizers before they "get to work".

I've seen TV reporters with a camera man in tow to take video clips that were shown later that evening on TV. It's another free way to get your organization's name in front of people. Make it a point to thank those from the media who attended your event (14.1).

Remember that fundraising is all about relationships. Create a relationship with the media. They are people like you. There is no unusual "mystique" about them. They may be busy, but so is every good business person. If your organization doesn't have a relationship with the press, start one. But start one early. Some newspapers have a society writer. Get to know that person. There may be a different weekend society writer. Get to know them all.

5.6   Advertising

Advertising plans can include:

- Public service announcements on the radio and TV

- Ads and feature articles in community newspapers and magazines
- Posters and fliers displayed throughout the area
- Billboards

Make sure you get on every newspaper, magazine, radio and TV community calendar, which is usually a free service. Try to get all of your advertising done for free. You do this by asking – and asking as early as possible. Just say, "We need your help."

Don't Count on Advertising to Sell Tickets

Remember this: Advertising generally will not sell tickets. It will only increase visibility, awareness and enthusiasm. The people who sell the tickets will be the board, staff, chairs, and volunteers. When someone is approached to buy a ticket, he or she might say, "Hey, I heard your advertisement on the radio," and may be more inclined to buy a ticket. Someone who has bought a ticket and then sees or hears an advertisement, might say, "Hey, I'm going to that," and they'll become more excited to go. But advertising seldom generates ticket sales in and of itself. People talking to people sell tickets (7.3).

Posters and Fliers

Posters and fliers are designed to be displayed on employee bulletin boards at businesses, and where the general public hangs out, such as libraries, grocery stores, restaurants and small businesses.

Posters come in all different sizes. See if you can get an artist to produce a painting to be used as a graphic on your poster. Then sell the original painting at the live auction. See Artwork Considerations (4.5).

5.7   Contact the media after the event

Contact the media within a day or two after the event. That would include local newspapers and magazines. Tell them the number of people who attended, how much you raised (these can be rough figures), celebrities and VIP who attended, etc. The publicity you get will serve to increase the visibility and awareness of your organization.

6. Printing Chair

6.1 Build a relationship with graphic designer

Consider selecting a Printing Chair who has experience with printing, graphic design or desktop publishing. A printer or graphic designer would make a good candidate.

If your organization doesn't already have a good relationship with a graphic designer, then you need to make one. By graphic designer, I mean a graphic design company, a printer with an in-house graphic designer, a public relations firm, or advertising agency with a graphic design department. A graphic designer can suggest all sorts of creative things to do with your Save-the-date postcards, posters, invitations, printed programs, etc. Ask them to donate their services. Consider these suggestions:

- Take two or three people and meet with the owner in person.
- Make your initial contact as early as possible. A year in advance is good.
- Offer something in return. When you ask someone to give you something, you need to be prepared to give something back. Refer to Decide on Donor Incentives (1.15) for ideas. Tell the owner that his or her design will be seen by hundreds of potential clients.
- Ask the owner if he or she would be interested in being on your organization's steering committee.
- If the owner will donate time but not material, see if you can get material at cost. And then try to get someone to underwrite the material.
- Offer to pay full price for specified printing needs if the printer will provide certain other specified printing needs at little or no cost.

Once you find a good graphic designer, set expectations right away. Determine the dates that you will need your designs for printing and put them in writing.

Sometimes when people agree to do something for free, they don't pay attention to deadlines. Paying customers tend to get served before non-paying customers. This can turn into a real problem if your deadline is approaching and your graphic designer doesn't consider you a priority. It is also harder to insist on corrections or ask for last minute changes if you are getting the printing done for free.

Regardless of whether or not you pay, make sure your graphic designer understands the importance of keeping deadlines and has plenty of advance notice.

6.2   Take care of printing needs

Build a relationship with a printer the same as you would a graphic designer (6.1). Here are some possible printing projects:

- Donor slips (4.2)
- Save-the-date postcards (7.2)
- Newsletters (5.2)
- Invitations (7.4)
- Advertising posters (5.6)
- Printed program (9.1)
- Direction signs (10.5)
- Sponsor banners (3.6)
- Table numbers (10.20)
- Table purchasers' names (7.5)
- Silent auction bid sheets (11.4)
- Live auction bid sheets (12.11)
- Live auction item numbers (12.3)
- Bid numbers (1.9)
- Displays, pictures, posters, and notes (10.6)
- Seating map (8.3)
- Post-event survey postcards (1.20)

7. Invitations Chair

7.1 Develop and update your mailing list

Anyone who has ever donated anything to your cause should be on your mailing list. Your mailing list should also include people who, at some point in their lives, have had an experience with what your organization is about. Imagine the following scene:

> Mary walks to her mailbox, reaches in, and grabs the handful of letters and ads. She sorts through them as she walks back to her front door, spending about 1 second on each piece of mail, deciding if she'll open it or chuck it. She flips to your invitation. How will you keep her attention? How will you get her to open it?

The thing that will make her interested in your piece of mail is the experiences she has had that give her a reason to care about what your organization does. If your organization works with cancer patients and her sister has had cancer, she will care about your cause. If your organization is about helping children with disabilities and her niece has a disability, she will care about your cause. If your organization is about helping preserve the environment or supporting the arts or helping the homeless and she has a link to that, she will be interested in what your organization does.

So try to develop a mailing list of people who have a reason to be interested in what your organization is about. Then when you have a ballroom, or a gymnasium or a tent full of guests who already have some sort of tie to your organization's purpose, you'll be ahead in the game in getting your guests to gain a desire to support your cause.

Also keep in mind that in order for people to open their purses and wallets at your event, they must have the ability to do so. If they are having trouble paying this month's bills, as much as they would like to help, they may not be able to, and throw away your invitation.

If there are people on your mailing list who have received an invitation year after year but have never attended, delete them. Don't waste another stamp on them.

Every once in a while send something by first-class mail to everyone on your mailing list. You will receive that letter back if the recipient has moved. Then you can take that person off your mailing list.

7.2 Send out "Save-the-Date" postcards

As early as 4 to 10 months before the event, send a "save-the-date" postcard to everyone on your mailing list and to the press. Make sure you send a postcard and not a letter. People can't resist reading postcards.

At the top of the postcard it should read, "Save This Date". Under that it should state:

- Your organization's name
- Date of event
- Time
- Location
- Theme (if you have decided on one)
- Financial goal
- Compelling reason why you are raising the money

Your postcard can be just plain text, or you can get creative. Some organizations use fancy graphics or include a peal-off sticker for a calendar. Sending out Save-the-date postcards will not only help people remember your event, but communicate that you are smart and well organized. Get this to the printer as soon as possible.

7.3 Give last year's bidders a personal call

The most effective way to get someone to come to your event is for them to get a personal invitation from a friend. Find out who your bidders were at your last event. Find out who invited them. Then have those people invite those guests again by visiting or calling them. Letters will not do in this case – too impersonal.

If that option is not possible, then have a VIP within your organization do the inviting. Perhaps the Event Chair or a member of the board or the Executive Director would be an appropriate person to assign.

This personal invitation should happen sometime between when the Save-the-Date Postcards went out and when the Invitations are due to be sent.

You want to have all the bidders from past years attend your event – and keep returning every year. If some good bidders missed the last event, don't hesitate to call them to say you missed them at the last event and invite them back to your up-coming event. Personal customer service is essential in maintaining and growing a good audience.

7.4 Send out invitations

This is the first impression of what is going to happen on the night of the event. Therefore, it is an important communication tool. The invitation should provide the following information about the event:

- Date
- Time
- Location (include a map if needed)
- Theme/Attire
- Ticket price
- How much we are going to raise
- The compelling reason for raising money
- Celebrity guest

- Silent auction, dinner, live auction, entertainment
- See Event Fact Sheet (1.12)

The invitation might also have these parts included:

- Stamp
- Outside envelope
- Invitation
- Response card to ask:
  - How many are coming
  - or do they want to reserve a whole table
  - or can they make a financial contribution because they are unable to attend
- Response envelope
- Map showing location of event
- DVD showing last year's party with a personal invitation by the Auction Chair

Mail the invitations first-class. Any invitations returned to you due to the intended recipient having moved will help you clean up your data base. Also, try to get the invitations done in-kind or underwritten.

Contact Collectors

If someone in your organization has procured a fabulous item that would appeal to collectors, try to contact those collectors. Items of worth to collectors would include wine collections, antique cars, antique furniture, artwork, jewelry, autographed photos, custom motorcycles, etc. There are clubs that collectors join that you can contact. There are magazines that cater to collectors in which you could advertise or from which you could get mailing lists.

The point is, if you have something that would be of great value to a collector, don't give it away to a non-collector. Find people who appreciate its true value and invite them to your event to bid on it.

7.5 Table purchases

When someone purchases a table, they get to invite their friends to fill the seats at the table. They get to sit together as a group. They also get recognition: a sign on the table with their name on it, and their name mentioned in the printed program and in the next newsletter. Table purchases will be made by three types of people:

1. Individual patrons
2. Corporations
3. Table Hosts (7.6)

Some organizers consider the value of these extra perks to be worth more than the total cost of single tickets to fill a table, so, they charge more for table purchases. How much more? Well, that varies, but I've heard of 33% and higher.

Consider making the provision on the invitation for a table purchase.

7.6 Table host party

As an Auctioneer I have had many opportunities to observe audiences during live auctions. I have noticed that the people who are having the most fun are usually those who are sitting with friends. Sometimes there will be a whole table of friends, laughing and joking and BIDDING. When I auction off an item like an Italian dinner for 10 people (5 couples), they pool their money and bid as a group.

When a table of friends has the bid, they applaud and yell. When they lose the bid to someone at another table, they all groan and grumble in unison. Then they get into a huddle and eventually someone's bid card will go up and they'll all hoop and holler again. When I get two tables of friends bidding against each other, it can be very entertaining – and profitable.

Sometimes two friends at a table will bid against each other for a single item. Their friendly rivalry is fun to watch and often causes the bidding to go high. The Table Host Party is an effective way to fill tables with friends.

The Venue

Six months before your event, arrange a gathering of people to come together at a distinctive place such as a celebrity's home, a luxurious estate, an exclusive country club, or an out-of-the-ordinary new building. Invite all of your best bidders and big spenders, major donors, community leaders, company CEOs, friends of your organization, friends of committee members and volunteers, and anybody you would like to see become a table host.

The venue should attract people. It should be the kind of place that people would love to get a glimpse of inside. A celebrity would also help to draw people. A celebrity can be a TV or movie star, a popular entertainer, a local radio or TV personality, a government official like a governor, mayor or senator, a well-known CEO of a corporation, or a local or national popular sports figure.

The Reception

From the moment your guests step into your Table Host Party, make them feel important. Greet them at the door. Introduce them to your board of directors, your executive director, and any celebrities that might be there.

Have a small reception period. Give them a tour of the place. Provide a nice display of refreshments such as: a fruit platter, shrimp platter, or a vegetable tray with dip; perhaps some crackers and cheese, and a variety of drinks. Use people's names when talking with them. Introduce them to one another. Then conduct a short meeting.

The Meeting

The purpose of the meeting is to (1) give a sneak preview of the event and (2) recruit Table Hosts.

The first part of the meeting is to tell everyone about the upcoming event. Describe the event including the date, time, theme, attire, location, how much you intend to raise, the compelling reason to raise the money, the celebrity guest, the entertainment, auction items, etc. It sounds a whole lot like the Event Fact Sheet (1.12), doesn't it? Make your event sound like THE place to be on that evening. This presentation should be relatively brief.

The second part of the meeting is to ask everyone to be a Table Host for your upcoming event. You'll need to know in advance how many people each table will hold (10.12). Say something like this:

"And now we want to talk with you about the 'Friendship Tables' we are going to have at our event this year. And we need your help. We would like to ask everybody here to become a 'Host' of a table at our upcoming gala. When we say that, what we're asking you to do is put your very best friends at your table. People that you enjoy spending time with. People you go to sporting events with, go on trips with, eat lunch with. What we're asking you to do is commit to fill the seats around your table with those best friends."

"Here's what we've discovered. People who have the most fun at our events are usually those who are sitting with friends. Sometimes a whole table of friends will pool their money and bid as a group on an auction item such as a day at the spa for 10 people."

"In addition to inviting your friends to sit with you at your table, we want you to buy each of your guests a gift. It can be as simple as a beautifully gift-wrapped box of chocolates, or as elaborate as a champagne or wine glass." Your gift should be whatever you want people to remember you by."

"Your table is going to be a mini-party; a tail-gate party you might say, at our gala, that you will host. You provide the friends; we provide the food, drink, entertainment, and items to bid on. You may want to do something crazy like all arrive together in a limousine. Maybe you'll want to get some rooms in the hotel and stay overnight and have a pajama party after the event."

"We like to think you're planning on attending anyway. And you'll probably bring another couple. So that means you only have to get three other couples. Five couples to a table."

"Now, because of your willingness to help make our gala the most successful ever, we will put a sign on your table with your name on it. Your name will appear as a Table Host in the printed program and you will be recognized in our next newsletter. And oh, by the way, if anyone at your table is a winning bidder, your entire table will be treated to champagne" (12.20).

"Are there any questions?" Answer any questions. Then ask, "So, everybody who can help us out by becoming a table host, please raise your hand."

Try to anticipate the questions your soon-to-be Table Hosts will ask. Consider these questions and possible answers:

Q: Do I have to buy a ticket if I am a Table Host?
A: We would never deprive a Table Host of buying a ticket.

Q: Can I request where I want my table to be?
A: We will take requests and do our best – but no guarantees.

Q: Can we get a discount on hotel rooms?
A: (Try to get the hotel to discount rooms. If that's not possible, try to find an underwriter.)

Wouldn't it be great if every year you could get more and more Table Hosts? Try this idea. Use more incentives for your Table Host. How about a photo opportunity for your table of friends with the celebrity that will be at your event? How about a free drink for Table Hosts and friends at the bar?

Don't assume that your new Table Hosts will do as they committed without reminders. Follow up. Get their contact phone number and call periodically to see if they have filled their tables. Don't forget to send a hand written thank-you note after your Table Host party. Send a thank-you note to even those who declined to be Table Hosts. They just might change their mind after they receive your kind thank-you note.

Find excuses to send Table Hosts updates about the event that will act as subtle reminders to fill their tables. For example, tell them about the fabulous items that you just got for the live auction. Tell them you found a limousine company that will give them a deep discount if they reserve their limousine by a certain date.

During the event, if you have the need to move all your guests from one area into the dinner area, make it a point, in your last communication with your Table Hosts, to ask them to go to the dinner area when invited. Where Table Hosts go, their friends go also, and the move to the dinner area will be faster.

Invitations Chair

8. Reservations Chair

8.1 Receive reservations

You will receive reservations from people who have received invitations in the mail. Add them to the guest list. You will receive reservations over the phone. Add them to the guest list. A board member or volunteer will ask you to add so-and-so to the guest list. Where's the guest list?

If you have a computer system with a guest database then you'll need to update that. You can also keep information about guests on a spreadsheet. You can use the same spreadsheet that is explained below (8.6). When you add a guest to your spreadsheet or database you can also assign a bid number and a table number if applicable.

The important thing is that you have some kind of system to keep track of all guests intending to attend your event.

You should be keeping another list or database of all people who have ever expressed an interest in your organization over the years. You'll use this database as a mailing list (7.1) to send out invitations every year. This mailing list will include names, addresses and telephone numbers. So make sure that both your mailing list AND your reservations list gets updated as reservations come in.

8.2 Staff the registration table

The registration table is where guests check into your event. It should be located just outside the entrance to your event. It is at this table where guests can:

- Present their names for admission to your event
- Buy admission tickets
- Receive the table numbers at which they will be sitting

- Receive their Printed Programs
- Receive their bid numbers

It is important that the registration line be kept short because guests do not like to wait in line. So, enlist enough people to work at the registration table to ensure that guests will get through registration quickly.

Train your staff in the registration process and show them how to handle occasional problems that might pop up, such as someone who said they bought a ticket but whose name does not appear on the guest list, or someone who wants to sit with another couple who has been assigned to a different table.

If your lines start to get long because you are requiring all guests to fill out contact information for your database, provide clipboards and pens to pass out to the people waiting in line. They can fill out the contact information while standing in line and simply hand it to the person at the registration table. That will help speed up the registration process.

8.3   Design seating chart

You need to prepare a seating chart only if you are planning to have reserved seating. See Reserved Seating vs. Open Seating (1.8). Coordinate the seating with the Party/Decorations/Entertainment Chair (10.22) who can tell you where the stage will be. Keep the following guidelines in mind:

- If you are aware of big spenders attending the auction, spread them out so they are sitting on both sides of the room. If big spenders are seated only on one side of the room, the Auctioneer pays little attention to the other side, which might leave some guests feeling ignored. Big spenders should sit closer to the front than the back.

- Put guests who you know will stay to the end of the auction on the front row in front of the stage. It is disconcerting to see people sitting close to the stage get up and leave before the live auction is over.
- The worst seats are those directly left and right of the stage, where speakers, entertainers, and Auctioneers seldom look. Put less-likely-to-bid people there.

Using Table Numbers

If you are going to use table numbers, make them big enough for the Auctioneer to read in case he or she needs to direct a Runner to the Table. Make them big enough for people who left their glasses home to find their table.

It can be frustrating for guests to be unable to find their table. And your mission is to eliminate frustration. Display table numbers so they all face the entrance of the room. If you are not using bid numbers, table numbers should face the stage so the Auctioneer can direct Runners to the tables.

Also, put tables in an easy-to-understand numerical order. If there are so many tables that it might prove challenging to find a particular one, create and display a table seating map (next topic).

Consider a Seating Map for Guests

I helped an organization that expected 900 guests. 90 tables were required to seat everyone. Just inside each entrance to the ballroom, on an easel, was displayed a seating map – a drawing of the room and where each table was located. Each table was identified by a number. Guests simply looked for their assigned table number on the seating map to locate their table. It saved a lot of unnecessary confusion.

You don't have to have 900 guests to need a seating map. You might consider using a seating map if you only have 20 or 30 tables. It's up to you.

Consider assigning volunteers to be hosts and hostesses and escort confused-looking guests to their tables. Be prepared to set up more tables if you sell tickets at the door.

8.4 Assign bid numbers to guests

Should you assign bid numbers to guests? Take a look at To Use Bid Numbers or Not (1.9). There you will learn the pros and cons of using bid numbers.

When should you assign bid numbers? In Receive Reservations (8.1), it is suggested that the bid numbers be assigned at the time reservations are made.

Where should bid numbers be recorded? As recommended in Prepare a Registration Spreadsheet (8.6), record bid numbers on the Registration Spreadsheet.

8.5 Prepare live auction bidding paddles

Bidding paddles are used only if you are going to assign bid numbers to your guests (8.4). As the Auctioneer calls for bids, people make their bids by raising their bidding paddles. That is, unless they nod, wave a finger, touch their cheek, tap their chest, or raise their hand to bid. I've even seen people bid by winking, in which case I say, "Sir, are you bidding or winking at me?"

You can make a simple bidding paddle by taping a popsicle-stick to the back of a stiff piece of poster board. Then write the bid number on the front side of the bid paddle *on a white background*. Make sure the number is big enough to be easily read from a distance. If you can cover the number with your fist, the number is too small for the Auctioneer to read from the stage.

I've seen bid numbers written on white paper plates at some informal auctions, which worked pretty well.

The most common bidding paddles in my experience are the printed programs (9.1). Simply use a *wide* marker to write the bid numbers on the back of everyone's printed programs. The back of the printed program should be white and the marker should be black.

When the Auctioneer sells an item, he will ask the winning bidder to hold up his or her bid number. Then he'll read the bid number for the Clerk to record. Did I mention that the bid number needs to be big enough to be easily read by the Auctioneer from across the room?

8.6   Prepare a registration spreadsheet

Use a spreadsheet program like Microsoft Excel to create a spreadsheet of guest information. I'll call it the Registration Spreadsheet. The column headings should include:

- **Attended** – This column will be left blank and will be checked off by the registration volunteers when the guests arrive and check in at the registration table.
- **Last Name/First Name** – list all guests for whom you have received a reservation.
- **Bid number** – the bid number assigned to that guest
- **Table number** – the table number assigned to that guest

The registration spreadsheet will be sorted in two different ways. The first sort will be by "Last Name" and a copy given to each volunteer at the registration table. As the guests arrive, they will give their names to one of the registration volunteers who will look up their names in alphabetical order on the spreadsheet and check the names off in the "Attended" column.

Following is an example of a registration spreadsheet:

Attended	Last Name	First Name	Bid Number	Table Number
	Ames	John	11	17
	Ames	Sue	11	17
	Baker	Tom	10	5
	Baker	Linda	10	5
	Call	Jamie	9	6

If there happens to be two couples with the same last name, make sure you get the right couples sitting together at the same table.

Assigning Bid Numbers to Couples

Notice in the spreadsheet above that couples share the same bid number. This serves to reduce the number of file folders the Cashiers will have to keep track of. The Cashiers will maintain a folder for every bid number. If couples share the same bid number, the number of folders will be cut in half.

If couples request separate numbers, have a list of unassigned numbers from which you can choose and assign. Remember to update the registration spreadsheet if that happens.

The second sort will be by "Bid Number" and a copy of that registration spreadsheet given to each of the silent auction volunteers. They will use their copies to notify silent auction winning bidders by looking up the bid numbers of the winning bidders, and determining the table number where the winning bidders can be found. Following is the same spreadsheet but sorted by bid number.

Attended	Last Name	First Name	Bid Number	Table Number
	Call	Jamie	9	6
	Baker	Tom	10	5
	Baker	Linda	10	5
	Ames	John	11	17
	Ames	Sue	11	17

8.7 Prepare packets for guests

A guest packet can contain any of the following:

- Printed program
- Name tag
- Bid paddle
- Party favor

Consider putting the guest packets at the tables rather than giving them to guests as they arrive. That way guests will remain unencumbered for carrying drinks and bidding on the silent auction. They will, however, need their bid numbers in order to bid on silent auction items.

8.8 Maintain a guest database

Maintain contact information including names, addresses and phone numbers of those who attend your event. This database will be used for sending thank-you letters, newsletters, and invitations to next year's event.

9. Printed Program Chair

9.1 Design the printed program

Printed programs, or "catalogs" as they are sometimes called, come in all different sizes. If your fundraiser has a dinner before the live auction, consider making your printed program long and narrow, making it easier to fit next to the dinner plate. If you use a spiral binder the printed program will lay flat when it is opened.

The printed program should, at the very least, contain (1) a description of the live auction items and (2) recognition of donors. I've seen printed programs list facts about the organization, list members of the organization, list members of the committee, list members of the board, include the evening's agenda, the dinner menu, the live auction rules, the silent auction items, display advertisements for donors, profiles on people who are going to speak, profiles on people being honored; the list goes on.

Many Printed Program Chairpersons put off designing the printed program until all of the auction items are in. That usually doesn't leave much time for designing the overall program. Start designing the program early, so you have plenty of time to accurately include all the information you want. Then when you know what the auction items are, just stick them in and you're done.

I would like to make some suggestions about printing the live auction items. Remember, we are marketing these items to potential buyers. So the easier each item is to read, and the more desirable we make each item appear, the more bidding we are going to generate. Consider the following:

- Number each live auction item in the printed program. The numbers should be in the same order as the live auction items on display. Coordinate with your Live Auction Chair.

- Consider describing one item per page.
- Make headings big, bold and descriptive – this is the attention getter.
- Make major features into bullet points so the eye can pick them out easily.
- Follow with a more detailed description to explain:
  - What it is
  - Where it is
  - When it is
  - When it expires
  - How to get there
  - For how many people
  - Important restriction
- Include the donor's name.
- Include the estimated retail value.

Make your headings descriptive. Your guests should be able to recognize what the item is when they read the heading. Here are some examples of good headings:

- Gourmet Dinner for Eight at Warner's Restaurant
- Round Trip Ticket for Two Anywhere JetBlue Flies
- Two Night Stay for Two at a Condo in Aspen
- Elegant Sofa

Here are some headings that I plucked out of actual programs that are examples of what NOT to do. Can you tell what they are trying to sell?

- Get it Together
- Spice Up Your Weekend
- Party On
- Up, Up and Away

People like to know from the heading what you are selling. They are used to reading newspapers with descriptive headings preceding articles. If the heading is too confusing, people may not read further, which may result in them not bidding.

Should you list the items on the silent auction? I don't think people pay much attention to a list of silent auction items. I say leave it out unless you have a good reason to include it.

Should you make the printed program easy to read? Why do I ask such an obvious question? Because I've seen too many printed programs that are not easy to read.

I once watched a guest pick up his program, open it, close it, toss it onto the table and say, "Need my reading glasses for that". Guests will be sitting in dim light, in a noisy room, having left their reading glasses at home, drinking, and trying to watch the auction. So make reading the program as easy as possible.

- No fancy fonts. I suggest using Times New Roman or Arial fonts. Most newspapers use Times New Roman because it's been shown to be easy to read in print. Most web pages are written in Arial font.
- No fonts smaller than 12 point, 14 point is even easier to read.
- Do not use all uppercase letters. I actually saw a program written in all uppercase letters. It was terribly hard to read. Don't ever let me catch you doing that.

Following are two descriptions of the same auction item. Which one attracts your attention? Which one would you rather read in a dimly-lit, semi-noisy, crowed room, without your reading glasses, after a few drinks?

Fun in the Sun

Enjoy a week-long vacation in one of Mexico's premier vacation spots, Puerto Vallarta. You will stay in a luxurious suite, which offers a breathtaking view of the magnificent Bay of Banderas. Experience three beautifully landscaped swimming pools, including one with a waterfall. Relax, sunbath, golf, see the sites, go horseback riding, try parasailing over the ocean, shop. Subject to availability. Must be used by December 31, 20xx. Book early for best availability.
Airfare for two included. Not good over the Christmas Holiday.
Velas Vallarta Grand Suite Resort
John and Mary Smith
Delta Airlines

3

Puerto Vallarta, Mexico

- 2 people
- 5 nights at Velas Vallarta Grand Suite Resort
- Airfare included
- Expires December 31, 20xx

Enjoy 6 days and 5 nights in paradise. Your luxurious suite offers a breathtaking view of the magnificent Bay of Banderas. Experience three beautifully landscaped swimming pools, including one with a waterfall. Relax, sunbath, golf, see the sites, go horseback riding, try parasailing over the ocean, shop. Subject to availability. Book early for best availability. Airfare for two is included. <u>Not valid during the Christmas holiday</u>.

Estimated retail value: $3,100

Thanks to:
Velas Vallarta Grand Suite Resort
John and Mary Smith
Delta Airlines

Did you even finish reading the first example?

The second item description, as you can see, requires less effort to read when compared to the first. The font is larger. The item is numbered. The heading stands out and is descriptive. The bullet items make the main features easily to understand. You don't have to read the whole thing to know what it's trying to say like you do with the first item description. The line that says, "week long" in the first example has been changed to "6 days and 5 nights", in the second example for clarity.

If the reader has any interest at all in going to Puerto Vallarta, he or she will most likely continue reading after the bullet items. The easier to read, the better – that is so important.

Make sure restrictions are noted. Here, the phrase, "Not valid during the Christmas holiday" is underlined to make this restriction clear to the buyer. You don't want someone to buy this item intending to spend Christmas in Puerto Vallarta.

The donors' names are set off in italics. This helps to visually separate the item description from the donor information. It also makes the donors feel good to see their names stand out. Did you notice the Estimated Retail Value is included? More on that in a minute.

Add Some "Sizzle" to Your Details

I occasionally see item descriptions that are boring, to put it bluntly. Spice it up with some interesting facts. You might have to do some research on the internet. The following is an example of a complete description, but a little dull. I have added some "sizzle" to this description in italics, to stir up some interest.

4

Steamboat Ski Resort Vacation

- 2 people
- 4 nights
- 3-day lift tickets
- 2 round trip airline tickets
- 20xx/20xx season

If you love to ski or snowboard, this is the package for you. Two of you will enjoy four nights in Steamboat Ski Resort in Colorado, along with two adult 3-day lift tickets. Round-trip airfare is included to Steamboat's regional airport.

For you snowboard lovers, Steamboat boasts having America's longest snowboarders "Super Pipe" at 650 feet long, 50 feet wide with 15 foot walls.

Steamboat also has a snowboard park that features an outdoor sound system and a variety of rails, sliders, rainbows, mailboxes, double-barrels, and a mini-version of the Super Pipe with 5-foot walls. This is truly a snowboarder's paradise.

For you skiers, try any of 164 ski trails.

Estimated retail value: $2,500

Donated by:
Steamboat Ski and Resort
Delta Airlines

Should You Publish the Retail Value?

You'll notice in the recommended item description examples above, that the estimated retail value of the item is published. I am often asked, "Should the retail value be published?" This is a debatable topic. Some say, that if the retail value is included with the item description, it may discourage people from bidding higher than retail value.

I have seen auctions where the bidding went right up to the published retail price and not a penny over. Getting retail is not a bad thing. If you can get retail on all your live auction items, consider yourself doing very well.

Some of your guests might know where they can get the item at a discount and only bid to the discount price. I've also seen auctions where the bidding went higher than the published retail value. That usually happens when the **The Four Objectives of a Successful Fundraiser** had been achieved. People don't mind bidding above retail value when they've been treated right and feel good about spending money with you.

There is another matter to consider. People who don't know the retail value might hesitate to bid high for fear of being "tricked" into bidding over retail. They just don't want to feel like they've been taken advantage of. People like knowing what retail value is. Then they can choose whether to bid under or over retail.

In my opinion, I find it best to print the retail value. If you cannot put a price on an item, such as an autographed football, simply value it as "Priceless".

Here is a word of caution. Don't be tempted to inflate the retail value of items. Some guests will know what the values are. If your published retail value is higher than true retail value, your informed guests will think you are trying to trick them into bidding higher, and feel you are taking advantage of them.

Should You Publish Minimum Starting Bids?

In the task entitled, Determine Minimum Bids (4.12), I discuss the pros and cons of using minimum starting bids. I don't think it is necessary to publish minimum starting bids with the description in the printed program unless every item has a firm minimum starting bid. If there are only a few minimum starting bids, it's not necessary to publish them.

Bid Numbers

Consider putting bid numbers on the back of the printed programs. You can use bid paddles or bid cards if you want, but for most events, the back of the printed program makes an adequate place to display the bid numbers. Make numbers big and bold by using an extra wide permanent marker. Bid numbers show up best when they are written on plain white backgrounds. The Auctioneer should be able to read any bid number from the stage. See To Use Bid Numbers or Not (1.9) for considerations regarding bid numbers.

Corporate Sponsors

Consider putting Corporate Sponsors (3.4) on the left-hand page of the printed program, and the live auction items on the right-hand page. It will give good exposure to your sponsors, and they will like that.

Leave Out Silent Auction Items

I don't think too many guests read the printed program to see what items are on the silent auction. They would rather just go look at the silent auction. So, if you want to save some time and money, leave the silent auction items out of the printed program. You should still acknowledge the silent auction item donors in the printed program.

Acknowledge Donors

Use your program to give thanks to anyone who has donated time or money. That would include:

- Chairpersons
- Committee members
- Providers of in-kind services (3.1)
- Underwriters (3.2)
- Cash contributors (3.3)
- Sponsors (3.4)
- Item donors (4.4)

Make Live Auction Items Easy To Find

When it comes right down to it, most guests open their printed programs to see what live auction items will be up for bid. You can make their search a little easier by putting the live auction items in the middle of the printed program where the program naturally opens. This requires a little more planning, but the extra effort will allow guests the pleasure of easily finding the live auction items.

9.2 Print the program

Consider having a graphic artist design the cover and a print shop print the cover. Then do the all of the inside design and printing in-house. It's one way to save some money.

Ideally, you want to get your printing done for free. Many graphic designers and print shops will help non-profits by providing free or deep-discounted services (6.1). But in order to make that happen, you need to form a relationship with the printer far in advance of the event.

Find out how early the printer needs to get the information for the printed program and let all the chairpersons know, so they can provide you with information they want included in the printed program before the deadline.

If you are fortunate enough to have the printing donated, be prepared to need long lead times because the job will not be as high a priority for the printer as if you were a paying customer.

10. Party/Decorations/Entertainment Chair

10.1 Overall look of the event space design

It will be your job to transform the venue into a party. Ideally, having everything in one room (silent auction, displays, banners, tables, stage, etc.) is best because it is very challenging to move a large group of people from one place to another in a timely manner. But you will not always have the luxury of keeping everything in one area. So, you work with what you have.

Try to visualize everything before you make it physically happen. Make everything work on paper first. Decide where everything is going to go. Try to think of all the problems that could possibly happen and determine the solutions. When you can see the party in your mind, and have transposed it onto paper – when you have a blueprint of how your event is going to look, then build it. The following tasks will help you get started.

10.2 Valet parking

Use valet parking to add a little class to your event. Use valet parking if you expect rain, or if your event is in a scary or dark area. Announce it in the invitation – not that it will be raining or scary, but that you intend to provide valet parking.

Make sure you have plenty of valet attendants at the end of the evening because people will be standing, holding their purchased auction items, waiting for their cars. Don't make them wait very long. This is the last impression they will have of your event. Make it a good one. Don't charge for valet parking.

Work with a professional valet parking organization. They have the experience, they're fast, and are trained in customer service.

10.3   Coat check

Guests will expect to find a coat check room if they wear a coat to your event. Providing a coat check is a way to pamper guests. Although coat check should be a free service, it would be considered appropriate to provide a large glass container in which guests can put in a dollar or two if so inclined. Prime the glass container with a few dollar bills to get coat check donations started.

10.4   Arrange for security

It's a shame that people steal. People have stolen auction items from unattended, unlocked trucks and cars. They have stolen from unattended rooms. They have stolen from silent auction tables and live auction display areas during events.

There are two ways to prevent items from being stolen. Either lock them up or assign people to watch them. Assign volunteers to watch over the silent auction tables and the live auction display area during the party. Make sure the volunteers wear something that identifies them as members of the event staff to give them credibility. Hire a uniformed off duty policeman or security person to watch over the auction items and stake out the Cashier area during checkout. The mere presence of a uniformed security person will help to avert any problems.

Also, if someone has had too much to drink and gets a little out of hand, it's nice to have a security person there to help if needed.

10.5 Direction signs and Direction People

Outdoor Direction Signs

If your event is at a location that presents the possibility of anyone getting lost, provide large direction signs along the side of the road. After placing the signs, drive past them, as if you were a guest that has never been to the venue, and make sure the signs are easy to spot and easy to read. Remember to collect the signs after the event.

Indoor Direction Signs

You should always display a sign with the name of your organization at the entrance of your event. If the entrance is not easy to locate from the parking lot, use direction signs to help guests find it.

If your event location is hidden inside a large building, such as a hotel or school, don't assume all guests know how to get to the ballroom or the gymnasium. Place signs at the entrance of the building and at every intersection in the hallways. If needed, use signs to guide people to stairs, elevators, coat check, restrooms, silent auction display area, live auction display area, dinner area, Cashier, etc. Confused and frustrating guests do not lend toward successful fundraisers.

Direction People

Assign volunteers as Direction People. Direction People stand next to the indoor direction signs. Their purpose is to welcome guests and direct them to the entrance of your event. They should be dressed in attire that ties in with your theme. Direction people add a personal (and pampering) touch to the directing process. I've seen two or more Direction People working in one location together; smiling, welcoming, directing, making guests feel important.

153

If people must walk a relatively long distance to the location of the event, you may want to provide a wheelchair to shuttle those who might have a hard time covering such a long distance on foot. In that case, one of your Direction People would push the wheelchair as a courtesy to your guests.

Direction People do not replace direction signs. At some point during the evening, after most of the guests have arrived, the Direction People will probably leave their posts for another assignment. The direction signs will remain in place to direct any late-comers.

10.6   Utilize education material

The second objective in **The Four Objectives of a Successful Fundraiser** is to give guests a desire to support your cause. The two ways of doing this are to educate them and make an emotional appeal. Displays, pictures, posters and notes are for educating guests.

Keep in mind that guests are not going to attend your fundraiser for the purpose of getting educated. They come to have a good time, and getting schooled in the virtues of your organization may not be their idea of a good time. So you have to educate them indirectly; educate them without them knowing they are getting educated. You need to be subtle.

Pictures are a good way to communicate what your organization does. After all, a picture is worth a thousand words, right? So educate your guests with displays, pictures and posters strategically placed in and around the reception area and silent auction tables. Put them anywhere people would wait in line. A short caption can be used to communicate any needed explanation, such as: "The new playground built with money raised at last year's gala."

I've seen pictures and posters stuck on walls with tape, only to fall off after an hour. So hang them in a manner that guarantees they will stay put. Displaying pictures and posters on easels works nicely.

154

Notes

Notes are small cards placed in strategic places with one thought written in large enough letters as to be easily read from a few feet away. I've seem them placed over water fountains, taped to bar counters, and hung above urinals in the men's restroom. (Hey, hotels place newspaper pages there to be read, so why not your notes.)

Here's an idea that works very nicely. Put a different note at each place setting at the dinner tables. If there are 10 seats around a table you will make 10 different notes to go around each table. At the top of each note say, "Please share this thought with the guests at your table." It's a good way for guests to start conversing with each other and a subtle way to educate them at the same time.

So what do the notes say? Well, they can give a statistic like how many people die from cancer every year, or how many babies are born with birth defects every day, or how many children go without food or permanent shelter right in your neighborhood; something that relates directly with your organization's reason for being. Your notes can reflect the good your organization has done, such as, "last year we constructed 20 wells to bring fresh drinking water to 10 villages."

Notes should be short, poignant and relate to the needs your organization addresses and the good things your organization does. They should be easy to read in a dimly lit room by people who left their reading glasses at home. That means large text.

The purpose of these displays, pictures, posters and notes is to give guests an idea of how important it is to raise money at the fundraiser they are attending. This subtle education joined with the Emotional Appeal, to be given before the live auction begins, is intended to make people feel generous during the time they spend at your event.

10.7   Registration table location and setup

The registration table needs to be in a location close to the entrance and be able to accommodate a line of people. Coordinate with the Reservations Chairperson (8.2). One or more tables will be needed to handle registering all the guests for the event as they arrive.

10.8   Entrance location, design and setup

If your event has a theme, it should be evident at the entrance to your event. If your theme is Hawaiian, then your entrance should look like Hawaii with foliage and Hawaiian music and greeters in Hawaiian clothing. If your theme is Hollywood then you might want a red carpet leading up to the entrance. Your guests should start to get into the party spirit as soon as they arrive at your entrance.

Whether you have a theme or not, a celebrity or VIP greeter should welcome guests as they arrive – as explained in task (1.17). Don't make your entrance a bottle neck. Advise your greeters to keep the guests moving so the line to the entrance is kept short.

10.9   Photos of guests

Get a backdrop that ties into the theme and take photos of couples. With today's digital technology, it isn't hard to produce those pictures at the event for guests to take home. Pictures are a wonderful memento that will remind guests how much fun they had at your event.

10.10   Silent auction location and tables

Location

Ideally, the location of the silent auction tables should be in the same general location as dinner. That is because moving a large crowd from the silent auction area to the dining area is like moving a large ship. It takes time to get it moving and when it does finally move, it goes real slow.

Tables and Table Coverings

Make sure you have enough tables to hold all the silent auction items without needing to squish the items too close together. Two feet of table space per item is a good rule-of-thumb for small displays; more space for bigger displays. If you have to transport tables, arrange for transportation to and from the event.

As part of our smart marketing plan, we need to make the silent auction items look appealing to the guests. Table cloths or linens with skirting will be more alluring than bare table tops.

Get with your Silent Auction Chairperson and find out if the silent auction will be closing in sections and whether each section will be distinguished by a different color. If that is the case, you can use colored table coverings or table decorations that will conform to the color of the sections.

10.11   Bars and liquor

Can you sell liquor? Check the local laws and ordinances regarding serving liquor at your event. It would be a good idea to do this before the location selection (1.6) is finalized. Do you need to get a special license or temporary permit? Is it required that you provide insurance in case of an accident involving one of your guests? In some places it is prohibited to serve alcohol after a certain time or on Sundays.

Liquor selection. You will need to make a liquor selection. This applies to hard liquor, wine and beer. Prices will vary depending on the brand.

Purchasing options. When purchasing the liquor you think you'll need, remember to make sure that all olives, cherries, nuts, mixers and juices are included in the price. You have some options when purchasing and providing liquor for your guests.

- **You pay for drinks**. Guests drink for free. The advantage is the guests will like it, and it is one way to pamper guests. The disadvantages are it can become very costly, guests might drink too much, and uninvited guests might drop in for the free drinks.
- **Cash bar**. Guests pay for their drinks. Your only costs would be the bartenders and perhaps someone to handle the money. You might not want the same person pouring drinks to handle the money. The advantage is you save money. The disadvantage is your guests pay for every drink and you lose the pamper factor.
- **Combine the two**. Give each guest one or two tickets, upon arrival, allowing them a free drink for each ticket. After guests have exhausted their tickets, they pay for drinks. The advantage is guests like the free drinks and the pamper factor kicks in. The disadvantage is the cost you incur for the drinks bought with tickets. So try to find one or more people to underwrite (3.2) the drinks.

How many bars? A rule of thumb is 1 bar for every 75 to 100 people. If you have more then one bar, separate them so as to spread the guests around. Remember, your guests will not like to wait in line for very long. Provide enough bars and bar attendants to keep lines short.

Provide non-alcoholic drinks. You need to accommodate people who do not drink alcohol but would like something to drink. Some people just feel more comfortable with a drink in their hand.

Provide transportation for inebriated guests. Consider having a plan ready to take care of guests that have had too much to drink. Perhaps a taxi standing by or a designated driver on hand would be in order.

10.12   Dinner table locations and setup

Coordinate with the Reservations Chair (8.3), who is in charge of assigning guests to tables. You will also coordinate with the caterer and the venue management as to the location and setup of the tables.

If you're renting tables and setting them up yourself, you'll need to arrange a troop of strong volunteers to deliver the tables, set them up, load them again at the end of the event, and return them.

Round tables are popular for seating guests at dinner. There are three basic sizes: 60-, 66-, and 72-inch rounds. Here are some guidelines to keep in mind if you going to rent tables:

- 8 people can comfortably sit at a 60-inch round table
- 8 – 10 people can sit at a 66-inch table
- 10 people can sit at a 72-inch table

10.13   Table-setting design and setup

A table-setting would include table cloths or linen coverings, napkins, flatware, silverware and crystal. Normally a caterer (10.17) takes care of these details, but not every event is going to use a caterer. If you are not going to use a caterer, then you need to be attentive to these details.

If your event is informal, you may instead have to make sure you have enough Styrofoam plates, plastic forks, paper cups, paper napkins, and plastic table cloths.

10.14 Party favors

Party favors are nice gifts given to guests for the purpose of pampering. The gifts should be something the guests will want to take home with them. Examples of party gifts I've seen include:

- Hawaiian lei (with a Hawaiian theme)
- Oriental fan (with an oriental theme)
- Corsages for ladies and boutonnières for men
- Lotion in individual sample sizes
- A CD containing music from the event's entertainers
- Chocolate with the organization's logo imprinted in the chocolate
- Coffee mug
- An autographed book written by one of the speakers

On my website I have listed a few websites I discovered that sell party favors, novelties, and gifts. Go to **www.LetsDoAnAuction.com/resources.htm**.

10.15 Menu selection

The type of food you serve will depend on your theme (1.5). A black tie affair may suggest salmon and/or steak, while a western hoe-down may imply barbequed chicken or ribs. Just remember this. Make your food appealing to the masses. *Do not experiment with strange or exotic dishes.* Keep the menu simple, warm and basic. Have an interesting variety of breads on the table in a big basket. Bread and butter are a good way to fill up your guests who come really hungry. Some people don't eat meat, so provide an alternative.

Food can be provided by a caterer, brought by guests (pot-luck style), or cooked and served by your staff and volunteers. However you decide to provide the food, make sure you have the adequate equipment, food preparation area, electricity, water, garbage, and cleanup facilities available. Make sure conditions are sanitary. Do local regulations require you to have a food handler's permit or other permit to prepare food at your event?

Serve two different kinds of deserts. That way couples can share each other's desert and it's more fun that way.

10.16   Served dinner vs. buffet style

I have found in most cases that a buffet style dinner takes more time than a sit-down-and-be-served dinner. If you do have a buffet style dinner, make sure there are enough stations to keep the lines short. People hate standing in a long line – especially for food. Guests should be able to get food from both sides of the buffet tables.

Some organizations provide an interesting twist on serving dinner. They invite chefs from around the area to set up booths and serve their specialties. There may be as many as 20 different restaurants represented. Guests go from booth to booth, taste testing, and by the end of dinner-time, they're full. This kind of dinner also gives opportunity to having a contest. Guests vote by secret ballet for their favorite restaurant and awards are given out.

If you are having a sit-down dinner, serve desert when the auction starts. If guests eat desert during the auction, it helps to keep them entertained.

10.17 Caterers

If you hold your event at a convention center, hotel or restaurant, the catering will probably be provided in-house. For other venues you can hire outside caterers. The reality of catering costs can surprise rookie organizers. Caterers do not come cheap. So try to find one or more people to underwrite (3.2) the catering. Ask for references from the caterer and do some reference checking before you make the final decision who to hire.

You should build a good working relationship with the catering manager. Together you will go over:

- Your budget
- Appetizers (10.18)
- Menu selection
- Special requests such as vegetarian meals
- Event location
- Food preparation and staging location
- Serving location
- Number of guests – thus the number of meals to prepare
- Served dinner vs. buffet style
- Table cloths napkins, flatware, silverware and crystal
- What time to start serving
- If wine is to be served and which to serve
- If coffee is to be served
- Total costs including tax and gratuity
- Whether or not volunteers will be served meals earlier in the day and what their meal will be.
- What to do if tickets are sold at the door and more people come than originally planned.

It is in the best interest of the catering manager to make your meal experience a success. The catering manager wants your repeat business and a good recommendation from you to other fundraising organizations.

When it comes to food selections, remember, it is not you for whom the food is meant, so make food selections that will appeal to the masses. Experienced caterers should have a pretty good idea of what appeals to most people.

Every detail to which you agree will be written on a Banquet Event Order (BEO). The BEO is the final say as to what will get done. *If it's not written on the BEO, it will not happen.* So double check the BEO and make sure it meets all of your expectations. Any changes need to be made as far in advance of the event as possible.

You will be asked to submit a *guarantee* number of meals three days in advance of the event so that the caterer can make the proper preparations. You will be obligated to pay for that number of meals. So you need to have your expected attendance nailed down by that time. If you are going to err, err on the side of overabundance of food and drink. Running out of food before all guests have been served is not good during a fundraising event. Mad, hungry guests tend to be less generous.

10.18 Appetizers served during social hour

Is it better to have appetizers served buffet style or served by roaming servers? Let's look at some advantages and disadvantages of each.

Buffet Style

Advantages: Less cost, no servers to organize.

Disadvantages: Guests tend to congregate around the buffet. Some guests (although probably not YOUR guests) will take as much food as they can fit on their plates because some people arrive absolutely starved. Some people might stand by the buffet table and "graze" during social hour. Instead of your silent auction getting all the attention, your buffet will be the center of attraction. Also, if there is a long line, people might feel impatient waiting.

If guests have a plate of food in one hand and a drink in the other, what hand are they going to write their silent auction bids with? Neither – not without first putting down their food or drink. This might discourage bidding.

People with a plate full of food also tend to want to sit down to eat rather than wander around the silent auction tables spending money.

Served by Roaming Servers

Advantages: There is no buffet to draw guests' away from more important attractions. A feeding frenzy is avoided. Guests circulate more. Roaming servers tend to make guests feel pampered. Guests have at least one hand to write with between appetizers. There is no line to wait in.

Disadvantages: Severs can add more cost to the catering. If you don't use a caterer then you must organize the servers and train them to be gracious.

Whatever you decide, make the appetizers bite-sized finger food and easy to pick up. No sloppy appetizers, please. Also, be sure to provide places for guests to leave their toothpicks or napkins.

10.19   Table centerpieces

Centerpieces don't have to be flowers. I've seen teddy bears, dried plants, candles, fruit, toy cars, vases and Styrofoam snowmen to name a few.

Make you're centerpieces creative so that they will be appealing to your guests. Then offer them for sale. Provide a designated area where centerpieces can be purchased for a particular price on a first come first serve basis. All a person needs is their bidding number. Identify the centerpieces with the table number. Announce the sale of the centerpieces in the program and over the sound system.

Be aware that tall centerpieces can inhibit guests from talking to each other across the table. Tall centerpieces also hinder the Auctioneer's view of the audience, so avoid them.

Helium filled balloons do not make good centerpieces. People will pop them or they will float to the ceiling and cause a distraction. The hotel management will not like your balloons lingering on their ceilings during their next event. Some hotels prohibit using helium filled balloons. Floating balloons also make it difficult for the Auctioneer and Bid Spotters to see hands go up when guests bid.

I've listed some websites that will give you ideas for centerpieces on my website: **www.LetsDoAnAuction.com/resources.htm**.

10.20   Table number display cards

Coordinate with the Reservations Chairperson (8.3) to find out if you are going to use table numbers. If so, be sure table numbers are put on the right tables. I've seen hotels and caterers use table number holders to display table numbers. You may have to invent or borrow something in which to display your table numbers.

10.21   Display table purchasers' names

If a person or organization has purchased an entire table, that person or organization's name should be displayed prominently in the middle of the table. The display should be an attractive sign, large enough to be read from three tables away. The sign is one of the perks that go along with a table purchase. The table sign acts to acknowledge the table purchaser and help guests find their table.

10.22   Stage location and setup

For small sit-down audiences of say, 100 people or less, a stage may not be necessary. But for larger groups, expect to use a stage so everyone has a good view of the speakers and Auctioneer. For very large groups of say, 500 people or more, consider broadcasting whatever is happening to large screens place around the room.

Stage Placement

There are three possible placements of a stage in a rectangular room. Let's look at the advantages and disadvantages of each:

1. **At one end of the room.** *Advantages:* The speakers and Auctioneer don't have to look from side to side so much because most of the audience is right in front of them. Fewer Bid Spotters (12.16) are needed because the Auctioneer can see most of the audience at one glance. *Disadvantages:* Guests in the back of the room, furthest from the stage, might feel left out. They also cannot see the stage area very well from so far away. People in the back tend to be talkative.

2. **On the side of a room.** *Advantages:* Guests in the back sit closer to the stage allowing them to see better. This arrangement also gives guests sitting in the back more of a feeling of being included. *Disadvantages:* The speaker and Auctioneer have to look side to side more to see the entire audience. More Bid Spotters are needed to help the Auctioneer see bidders.

3. **In the center of the room.** *Advantages:* More people can sit closer to the stage than either of the other two arrangements, allowing them to see better and making them feel more included. *Disadvantages:* Microphone wires need to be strung through the audience (unless wireless microphones are used), making them a possible tripping hazard. The speakers and Auctioneer must turn all the way around to see the entire audience. The Auctioneer does more spinning around to receive bids, and cannot easily walk around within the audience. More Bid Spotters are needed than with either of the other two arrangements. If Bid

Spotters don't do a good job, bids can be missed, money lost, and some guests sent home unhappy. Speaking from an Auctioneer's point of view, a stage in the middle of a room poses the greatest challenge.

Stairs and Ramps

If a woman is expected to be on stage, and if that stage is so high that a woman in a skirt would have a challenging time stepping up to the stage, be sure to have stairs leading to the stage. If a person in a wheel chair is expected to be on the stage, a ramp to the stage will become necessary.

Stage Backdrops and Props

You may want to decorate your stage to go with your theme by using stage props and/or a stage backdrop.

I was at an event where the theme was "Under the Sea". The stage backdrop was a huge under-water scene. Then there were Mylar helium filled balloons in the shape of fish floating at different heights on each side of the backdrop.

Another event I attended was a tropical theme. The stage backdrop was a tropical beach and the front of the stage was filled with foliage.

On my website I've listed some websites that you can visit if you want to rent a stage backdrop. Go to **www.LetsDoAnAuction.com/resources.htm**.

10.23   Easels

Easels are used to display:

- Signage such as direction arrows or sponsor names
- Posters that represent auction items such as vacation destinations
- Paintings and prints to be auctioned off

- Item numbers during the live auction (12.10).

10.24 Podium and microphone stand

If there are going to be speeches, presentations or recognitions, a podium serves as a good solid object for people to hold on to, and a good place to put their notes. A podium is also a good place for the Item Describer (12.14) to keep his or her notes. Sometimes the Item Describer will need to write something down and it's nice to have a podium for that.

If the podium is going to share the stage with a dance performance or other form of entertainment, it will probably get in the way and have to be moved off the stage and then returned to the stage later. Make arrangements *in advance* for some muscle-men to move that podium on and off the stage.

If you are not going to use a podium, make sure there is a microphone stand present so speakers can use both hands during their presentation, rather than having to hold a microphone with one hand.

The Auctioneer will not use a podium or a microphone stand, unless you want your audience to go to sleep. The Auctioneer will be moving around with his or her microphone.

10.25 Sound system

A good sound system is critical to the success of your event. A sound system is like a referee. No one notices a good one, but everybody complains about a bad one.

No one will come up to you at the end of your event and say, "Hey, good sound system, man." So you ask yourself, why not skimp a little; save some money and go cheap on the sound system? I'll tell you why. You've invested too much work and expense to have it all ruined by a bad sound system. And a bad sound system will kill your event. I've seen it happen.

I have seen karaoke machines used as a sound system for audiences much too large for everyone to hear. I've seen one small speaker ineffectively used to cover a huge room full of people. I've had cheap sound systems go out on me. I've used sound systems so muffled and fuzzy, members of the audience shouted complaints. I've used sound systems set up for performing bands. The speakers were big all right, but in order for the guests in the back of the room to hear, the volume had to be turned up so high that it caused the guests sitting near the speakers to be blasted away. If there's one thing you do not want to pinch pennies on, it's the sound system. Please consider the following guidelines:

- Don't assume if your event is going to be held in a fancy hotel, that the house sound system will be good. Sometimes it is, sometimes it isn't.
- Rent sound equipment from a reputable company. Ask other organizations for referrals. Look in the Yellow Pages under Audio – Visual Equipment – Rent and Lease. Consider renting a sound man along with the equipment to set up and trouble shoot.
- Tiny speakers lose their sound quality when the volume is increased. Make sure your speakers are big enough to handle the volume needed.
- Speakers should be as high off the ground as possible. There are tripods made to hold speakers above the crowd.
- If you use a tripod, make sure it will not tip over. I've seen them tip over. You can use heavy sandbags to keep them from tipping.
- Cover wires with duct tape to prevent anyone from tripping. I've tripped.
- One speaker might work for a small crowd, but I always suggest at least two speakers because the sound quality is better.
- For a medium-sized crowd, say, up to 150 people, closely grouped, sit-down, (with 10 people to a table

for a total of 15 tables), indoors, in a no-echo room, two speakers might do.

- For larger crowds, put two speakers in the back of the room as well as two up front. You may have to use even more.
- Remember, gymnasiums echo. Advise anyone speaking to slow down and speak clearly.
- Test your sound system well before the event. It will probably need to be louder when the room is filled with people. So know how to adjust the volume. I once did a sound check before an event started and it sounded great. But when it came time to use my microphone for the live auction, there was a lot of irritating feed back. I asked the Item Describer to turn off his microphone and the feedback went away. We never did a sound check with both microphones on.
- Have someone familiar with the sound system be close by at all times in case something needs adjusting or goes wrong.
- Speakers outside do not project as far as they do inside.
- If your event is going to be **outside**, plan for electricity and extension cords.
- If your event is going to be **inside**, plan for electricity and extension cords.

Microphones

- Use two microphones: One on the podium for the announcements, speeches and Item Descriptions (12.14), and one for the Auctioneer. One microphone is sufficient but it requires passing it back and forth which can be a little awkward.
- Use a wireless microphone for the Silent Auction Emcee (11.1) and the Auctioneer if one is available.

There are three common types of microphones you should be aware of:

1. **Hand-held wired**. These are adequate for use at the podium. The Auctioneer can also get by with one, although it will restrict his or her movement.
2. **Hand-held wireless**. As an Auctioneer, I prefer a hand-held wireless because I don't have to keep flipping the cord out of my way. I can also roam through the audience if I choose. However, hand-held wireless microphones are usually more expensive to rent. They will also stop working if the 9-volt battery inside the handle goes dead – which has happened to me on occasion. So make sure, if you use a hand-held wireless, that there is a fresh 9-volt battery handy in case one is needed. You may be better off to replace the battery with a new battery before the event begins.
3. **Lavaliere**. These are small microphones that clip onto one's clothing with a wire that runs to a card-deck-sized unit that clips onto one's waste – or somewhere. I've never liked lavaliere microphones because I cannot vary the distance from my mouth to the microphone, making it hard to talk to someone without broadcasting my conversation.

10.26   Screens and projectors

Screens and projectors will be used if you are going to do a slide or video presentation.

If you are fortunate enough to know someone who can put together a professional video presentation about your organization, have him or her produce a five to eight minute presentation and show it just before the live auction. If you don't know someone who can do this, get busy and find someone because a video presentation can really evoke emotion and cause people to feel generous.

The next step down from a video presentation is a PowerPoint presentation. PowerPoint is one of the programs found in Microsoft Office. It's easy to learn and can be used to produce a nice slide show with music to go with the pictures. I've seen PowerPoint presentations bring an audience to tears. And along with tears come their willingness to open their hearts and wallets.

If you plan on using a video presentation you will need to plan on a projector and a screen on which to project. These items can be pretty pricy to buy, so you may want to borrow them from another organization or rent them from an audio/visual business. If you rent, try to get the business to donate as an in-kind service (3.1).

Get to know your audio/visual equipment intimately so you can trouble shoot any problems during the event. Set up the equipment early and make sure everything is working properly long before guests arrive. Remember to plan for electrical outlets and extension cords. Cover all electrical cords with duct tape to prevent anyone from tripping.

10.27 Display of live auction items

I've been to auctions where there was no printed program and the live auction items were not on display. Consequently, the guests had no idea what was going to be sold at the live auction until the live auction began. The items would then be described and auctioned off. The audience had only a few seconds to decide if they wanted any of the items bad enough to bid on them. Needless to say, the items didn't bring in as much as they could have if proper marketing had been done.

This is an extreme example but illustrates the need to do some marketing before the live auction begins. The third objective in **The Four Objectives of a Successful Fundraiser** is to get people to want what you're selling. You accomplish this by applying proven marketing techniques. The following marketing techniques will help to get people in the mood to pay top dollar for the items you worked so hard to procure.

172

- Display all live auction items in one place. Do not scatter them around the room or amongst the silent auction items.
- Identify the live auction items with a big sign that reads: "Live Auction". I've seen signs that were three feet high and eight feel long and some that were smaller. Just make it easy to see.
- Have the Silent Auction Emcee (11.1) announce the location of the live auctions items. The idea is to get everyone to go over and look at them.
- Number each item.
- Display items in numeric order. The order should correspond with the order in which the items are printed in the program.
- Display something for every item. This is meant to attract people's attention. If you cannot display the actual item, display something that can represent it. If the item is 18 holes of golf, display a putter and some golf balls. For a cruise through the Caribbean, display a poster, a pair of sunglasses and a bottle of suntan lotion. Get creative.
- Supply a description of the item in big enough letters so guests can read it without having to bend over to get closer.
- Before the live auction begins, move the items near the stage so the Item Displayer (12.13) will have easy access to them. Make arrangements in advance for movers to be on hand at the proper time.

10.28   Display of sponsor banners

The Underwriters Chairperson will make arrangements for sponsor banners (3.6) to be printed. It is your job to see that they get hung and presented well. Hang them behind the stage, over the silent auction items, anywhere they have good visibility.

10.29   Decorations

Decorations should compliment the theme (1.5) of your event. I've seen walls, ceilings, even restroom entrances decorated. I'll suggest three locations where you should consider having decorations.

1. Centerpieces on each dinner table. See Table Centerpieces (10.19).
2. At the entrance. See Entrance Location Design and Setup (10.8).
3. On the stage. See Stage Location and Setup (10.22).

10.30   Lighting

Lighting in the room needs to be dark enough to set the mood, but light enough so people can read their programs. During a video presentation, the lights need to be turned down a little more. During the live auction, lighting needs to be turned up enough to allow the Auctioneer to easily see bidders among the crowd.

Find out where the house lighting controls are located and assign someone to make the proper adjustments at the right times.

If you use a spotlight, do not put a spotlight on the Auctioneer. A spotlight on the Auctioneer will cause him or her to see a sea of blackness instead of bidders.

10.31   Temperature and ventilation

Rooms that are too hot or too cold will cause your guests to be uncomfortable. This does not lend toward pampering. It might be considered anti-pampering. Be aware that when people fill a room, the room temperature will go up due to all the warm bodies. When the sun goes down, the air may cool off. Be able to control the heat and/or air-conditioning at your event.

If you anticipate the temperature rising due to body heat, candles, spotlights and the like, consider cooling the room earlier to the point that when people enter the room, it will feel a little on the cool side.

10.32   Restrooms

Be sure your guests have access to restrooms and that the restrooms will be well stocked with toilet paper, soap, and paper towels. If your venue is outdoors, you may have to rent two or more portable outhouses (one for males, one for females). Assign someone to occasionally check the restrooms for tidiness and paper supplies.

Remember that people do not like to wait in lines – especially restroom lines. Plan ahead to keep lines short.

10.33   Garbage cans if needed

Make sure there are enough garbage cans for everyone's paper plates, cups and napkins if needed. Don't you hate it when garbage cans overflow and junk gets scattered all over the ground? Be sure to find out in advance where to empty those garbage cans and don't let them run over.

10.34   Entertainment

Unless you can get entertainment for free or have it underwritten, don't spend a lot of money for entertainment. There are probably some exceptions to that rule, but for the most part, you can get good entertainment without breaking the bank.

Go to the music department at colleges and universities. They can provide a variety of wonderful entertainers who would be happy to get the exposure and experience your event would provide them. Entertainment can come in many forms:

- Videos
- Live music – solo, quartet, band, or orchestra
- Disc jockey
- Dance performances
- Musical performances
- Children's choir (professional or otherwise)
- Guest/celebrity appearances
- Magician
- Barbershop quartet
- Parade
- Marching band
- Singers
- Lip sync entertainers
- Celebrity look-alikes
- Fashion show
- Entertaining speaker
- Comedian

Here are some things to keep in mind when looking for entertainment.

- Ask other organization for recommendations.
- Ask the entertainers for references – who they have worked for. Make some calls to those people and ask how they like the entertainers.
- Find out from the entertainers what equipment they will provide and what equipment they expect you to provide. Lighting and sound equipment are two important considerations.
- Make sure you and the entertainers understand and agree on the total cost, when the entertainers are to setup, rehearse, perform, and end their performance.
- Ask the entertainers what their policy is when asked to entertain longer than expected. I've seen musicians upset because dinner was delayed and they were asked to continue entertaining past the agreed upon ending time.

- Will the entertainers be invited to dinner? Can they bring guests? Make sure expectations are set.
- When the entertainers are from out of town, you may be expected to pay for their air travel, ground transportation, hotel and food – for them AND their entourage. Find out all the costs involved.
- Get everything in writing.

10.35   Arrange for first aid

It may never happen to you. You may never be faced with a situation where one of your guests requires first aid or CPR. But if the occasion presented itself, wouldn't you be glad if you had arranged for someone who was skilled in first aid and CPR to be at your event?

10.36   Organize the prize drawings

Some people call this a raffle. But since a raffle is considered a form of gambling in some states, and therefore illegal, I will refer to it as a drawing. Have volunteers distribute tickets for a "suggested donation" during cocktail hour, dinner, and up to the time of the drawing. Prizes can be one or many and can be given away at the beginning, middle and end of the live auction.

The prizes don't have to be expensive, although expensive is okay. People just love it when their name is drawn from a hat or bowl or spinning cage. Everyone applauds and they get a moment of recognition. However, when the event is over and you're counting the money from your drawings, you may discover that the drawing didn't generate a whole lot of money. They are fun, but are not usually a major money-maker. You have to ask yourself, "Can I raise more money by selling an item in the auction or by selling tickets to a drawing?"

You should comply with your state regulations to keep your drawing within the law.

Oh, by the way…why not conduct a drawing where everyone stands a chance to win without having to buy a ticket. In other words, draw bid numbers. Everyone has an equal chance to win. This is a fun activity you can do during the live auction to add a little extra excitement and entertainment.

10.37   Mini-store setup

The purpose of a mini-store is to provide another reason for guests to spend money. If you are a humanitarian organization, you might consider selling goods made by the people who benefit from your efforts. If you are the Red Cross, consider selling first-aid kits. Does your organization have tee-shirts, hats or mugs that can be sold? Think of something to sell that relates to your mission.

10.38   Lost and found

Inform everyone working at the event where the lost-and-found will be. Then, anyone finding a lost item will know where to take it, and everyone will know where to direct guests who have lost something.

10.39   Cleanup

Save all the Printed Programs. They can to be used as a sales tool for next year's event. Assign as many volunteers as you can to go around and collect them. Ask the caterer not to throw them away.

Assign all available volunteers to help with clean up.

11. Silent Auction Chair

11.1 Find a good silent auction emcee

A Silent Auction Emcee (Master of Ceremonies) is an enthusiastic person, who is not afraid of a microphone. He or she broadcasts important information and alerts guests to good deals during the silent auction:

> "Ladies and gentlemen, welcome to our event. There are refreshments being served and the bar is now open. Dinner's about 50 minutes away. And the chef has done a great job. You're not going to believe it. The Silent Auction is open and by the way, there is a bicycle in the blue section with only a $50.00 bid on it...worth about $250.00. And, in the green section a dinner for two worth $60.00, with only – are you ready for this? A $25.00 bid on it."

The Silent Auction Emcee closes the silent auction in sections, and does a countdown before closing each section: "Just 5 minutes to go on the blue section...1 minute to go on the blue section...10 seconds to go...9,8,7,6,5,4,3,2,1...the blue section is now closed...the green section will close in just 2 minutes."

Since the Silent Auction Emcee will be walking around making announcements, it's a good idea to provide him or her with a wireless microphone. The Silent Auction Emcee:

- Welcomes guests
- Announces the evening's agenda
- Announces the location of food, drinks and games
- Lets guests know how long until dinner

- Alerts guests to good silent auction deals
- Directs guests to the live auction items on display
- Closes the silent auction in sections using a countdown

Ask your Silent Auction Emcee not to drink until after the silent auction closes. Assign a silent auction volunteer to help locate items that need plugging.

11.2   Setup silent auction tables

Depending on the number of items you have, divide your silent auction into sections. Each section would be comprised of one or more tables. Distinguish each section with a different color. Use balloons, colored table cloth, colored bid sheets, or a combination thereof, to identify the different sections.

Sections can also have a theme. For example, you may have sections that are for:

- Toys
- Sports equipment
- Electronics
- Vacations
- Home
- Garden
- Camping

11.3   Display of silent auction items

The way a silent auction item is packaged will make a difference in how much attention it will get. Use creative ways to draw people's attention.

As guests walk past the silent auction items, they may spend only one or two seconds inspecting each item before moving on to the next unless there is something displayed to catch their attention.

Try to display something for every silent auction item. If the actual item can be displayed, then display the actual item. If the item is a certificate, don't display the certificate. Keep it in the envelope. People rarely stop to read an entire gift certificate. If a certificate is for dinner at a Chinese restaurant, for instance, display chopsticks. If it's for a round of golf, display golf balls and tees. If the item is a vacation, get a poster from a travel agency.

Write the item description on the Silent Auction Bid Sheet (11.4) or on an easy-to-read display card.

Items can be sold in a silent auction as a separate item, or in a bundle with other items. If you have many small items, you may want to bundle them. Put them in a wicker basket or other eye-catching container. I've seen wagons full of items and sold as a bundle including the wagon. On the silent auction bid sheet, list everything that the bundle contains.

Each item should be numbered. The number should match the number on the bid sheet that goes with that item.

11.4   Design and printing of the bid sheets

One bid sheet should accompany every silent auction item. Your guests will bid on the silent auction items by writing either their names or their bid numbers on the bid sheets along with the amount of their bid. When the silent auction closes, the people who wrote down the last bid (which should also be the largest amount) win the corresponding items.

Once the silent auction is over, it is necessary to inform the winning bidders of their good fortune. Unless they are informed, they might not know their bid was the highest, and leave without paying or collecting their winnings. The Cashier should also be informed of the winning bidders (11.19).

In the following example, I am going to explain how to use 2-part bid sheets for your silent auction. One part will go to the Cashier, and one part will be delivered to the winning bidder as a receipt.

You will make one bid sheet for every silent auction item or bundle (11.3).

On the bid sheet you will write a description for each item. The description should be written in a Times New Roman or Arial font, and the font size should be big enough to be easily read without having to bend over. To see an example of a good description, take a look at Design the Printed Program (9.1).

If the description requires more room than you have on your bid sheet, then it will be necessary to provide a separate piece of paper or card stock on which to display your description. If your item is a gift certificate, don't display the certificate; display an easy-to-read, well written description instead.

Consider each of the following items to be included on each bid sheet:

1. **Item number** – This is a unique number used to identify and retrieve the corresponding silent auction item.
2. **A bold heading describing the item**. Instead of "An Evening to Remember" it would be better to say, "Dinner for 2 and a Night at the Marriott". It should be understandable at a glance.
3. **Bullet items** describing all the cool features.
4. **Further description**, if needed, can be as creative as you like.
5. **Estimated retail value** (fair market value). The Fair Market Value is important for the winning bidder who wants to figure his or her purchase into this year's tax return.
6. **Donor's name** to give the donor proper recognition
7. **Starting bid**. This should be one forth to one third of retail value.

8. **Minimum raise (bid increments).** Use smaller increments for less expensive items and larger increments for more expensive items.
9. **A place to put bid numbers** or names and how much they are bidding.
10. **Consider pre-written bid amounts.** I've seen Silent Auction Bid Sheets that had bid amounts already written on each line in predetermined increments. The bidders only needed to write down their bid numbers. This way, bidders could not write bid amounts lower than the minimum raise.
11. **Optional guaranteed purchase.** This is for the bidder who doesn't want to keep coming back to raise the bid. The guaranteed purchase price should be higher than the retail value. Any bidder who writes his or her bid number in the Guaranteed Purchase box is guaranteed that item and does not have to return to bid again. The bidding is essentially closed for that item.

Following is an example of a silent auction bid sheet.

Silent Auction Chair

Item # _____   St. Mary School Benefit Gala, May 18, 20xx

Dinner and Marriott Hotel Get-Away

- Dinner for 2 at the New Yorker Downtown
- One night's stay at the Hilltop Marriott

Enjoy a fabulous dinner at the restaurant named "Best New Restaurant – 20xx" by City Magazine and then enjoy secluded privacy in a VIP room with a Jacuzzi.

Donor: New Yorker Downtown and Marriott Hotel

Value: $400

Starting Bid: $ _____   **Minimum Raise: $** _____

Bid #   **Bid Amount**

_____

_____

_____

_____

_____

_____

_____

_____

_____

_____

_____

_____

_____

_____

_____

_____

                                            $425.00
Guaranteed Purchase - Enter your Bid # here, and it's yours for the price posted

11.5   Provide a pen for each bid sheet

I attended a silent auction where there were no pens. It's hard to write down a bid without a pen. Don't let this detail slip through the cracks. Each bid sheet should have a pen next to it. Hotels may be willing to donate pens.

I worked with an organization that distributed pens they used at a silent auction the year before. Come to find out, the pens were all dried up. Check your pens prior to the event to make sure they still write.

Do not use pencils. Bids written in pencil are too easy for jokesters to erase and too easy for serious bidders to change in order to keep prices low.

11.6   Sound system

The silent auction needs a sound system for the Silent Auction Emcee (11.1) to use. Please refer to Sound System (10.25) for important information regarding your sound system.

11.7   When to close the silent auction

When should you close the silent auction? There are four possible times:

1. **Just before dinner begins**. I find this option to work best because it allows the silent auction volunteers time to process the silent auction bid sheets and notify the winning bidders before the live auction begins. Sometimes bidders like to know how much money they have left to spend on the live auction. This also gives bidders peace of mind, knowing that they don't have to jump up during dinner to check bids. This option, however, provides the shortest amount of time in which to keep the silent auction open for bidding.

2. **Just before the live auction begins**. I find this option to work second best. It allows more time to keep the silent auction open, but doesn't allow enough time for silent auction volunteers to process the silent auction bid sheets before the live auction begins.

3. **After the live auction ends**. This option obviously allows the silent auction to stay open the longest. However, it's been my experience that when the live auction is over, most people are done spending money and want to go home.

4. **During the live auction**. In my opinion, this option is the least preferable of the four suggested here. I would go so far as to say that it generally is a bad idea. When you make the announcement during the live auction that the silent auction is about to close, expect people to get up and leave the live auction to check on their silent auction bids.

11.8   How to close the silent auction

The decision of when to close the silent auction is based on the amount of items in the silent auction. For a small silent auction that only takes up one or two tables, I recommend closing it all at once.

In the case of a larger silent auction composed of many items and requiring several tables, close the silent auction in sections. By doing so, bidders who didn't get the item on which they were bidding in a closed section, have more money to bid on items in the remaining open sections.

I suggest allowing only two minutes between section closings. Two minutes creates more of a sense of urgency than say, five or ten minutes between section closings.

When closing the silent auction, don't surprise everyone by saying, "The silent auction is now closed." Give a ten minute warning, a five minute warning and a one minute warning. Then do a count-down for the last 5 or 10 seconds:

"The blue section will close in 10 seconds, 9-8-7-6-5-4-3-2-1-0. The blue section is now closed. Drop your pens and slowly step back from the blue section. Please give your attention to the green section as it will be closing in just two minutes."

11.9   Gather silent auction bid sheets

As soon as the silent auction closes (or a section of the silent auction closes), the volunteers should quickly gather the silent auction bid sheets before anyone can sneak in a bid after the buzzer. If two or more people are fighting over an item, you can do one of two things:

1. Conduct a mini live auction where just the interested parties bid against each other.
2. Give each party a piece of paper and a pen. Tell each to write his or her name, and the highest amount they are willing to pay. Gather the secret bids and announce the winner.

Your bid sheets should be at least two-part carbonless forms. Here's what to do. After gathering the bid sheets, separate them into two piles. Part-one of each bid sheet goes in one pile; part-two of each bid sheet goes in another pile.

Deliver the part-one pile to the Cashier volunteers. They will put each bid sheet in a folder corresponding to the winning bid number. The winning bid number will be the last and highest bid, or course.

Deliver the part-two pile to the winning bidders. How will you know where to find them? You will be given spreadsheets prepared by the Reservations Chairperson containing all your guests' names, bid numbers, and table numbers. Refer to Prepare a Registration Spreadsheet (8.6).

Your spreadsheets will be in bid-number order. Simply locate the winning bid number on the spreadsheet, find the table number and write it on the bid sheet. Now you know the table number at which the winning bidder is sitting.

Have the silent auction volunteers go to each winning bidder's table and ask for the person with the winning bid number to identify him or herself. Then present that person with their winning bid sheet.

Not Using Bid Numbers?

You must somehow inform your winning bidders so they know to pay for the item(s) they have won. I've seen winning bidders notified by:

- Announcing their names over the public address system – this works best for smaller silent auctions
- Posting notice on white boards or black boards
- Creating a PowerPoint slide to display on a big screen

12. Live Auction Chair

The live auction should be good entertainment for all of your guests whether they are bidding or not. Bidders, or course, will be entertained because they will be caught up in the thrill of bidding. But what about the guests who are not bidding? If the auction is not entertaining to them, they will turn to other forms of entertainment, like chatting, or worse, leaving. Chatty audiences can get so noisy that it becomes difficult for interested parties to hear the auction. At real boring auctions, even dinging a water glass with a spoon to get everyone's attention has little effect on the chatter level.

The more entertaining you make your live auction, the more well behaved your audience, the longer they stick around, the more generous they feel, and the better the chance of them returning to your event next year. Any one of these results would merit putting some effort into adding entertainment, or "show-biz", to your live auction. The following tasks will help you do that.

12.1 Find a good Auctioneer

The Auctioneer is very important to the success of your live auction. If you don't know a good Auctioneer, call other organizations that hold fundraising auctions and ask for recommendations. If someone has had a good experience with an Auctioneer, they are usually pretty glad to share the Auctioneer's contact information. Most people are also eager to share warnings about hiring certain bad Auctioneers.

People react differently to the different styles that Auctioneers use when calling for bids – whether they be professional Auctioneers or not. Some styles can be boring and uninspiring – even irritating and insulting. After all the work you've put into this event, you want an Auctioneer who can get the highest bids and be entertaining without being obnoxious.

It would be a good idea to attend an auction where a recommended Auctioneer is performing. By doing this, you can decide how well this Auctioneer will fit in with your group of guests. If someone recommends an unfamiliar Auctioneer to you, contact the Auctioneer and ask for names of other organizations for which he or she has worked. Call those organizations and ask their opinion of that Auctioneer.

Agree on a fee before you hire your Auctioneer. A simple written agreement may not be a bad idea. You can require the Auctioneer to attend certain meetings, arrive at the event by a certain time, etc., if you feel it necessary.

Do celebrities make good Auctioneers? Do professional Auctioneers make good *Fundraising* Auctioneers? How about free Auctioneers who dabble in auctions? The answer to these questions is, some do and some don't. Use the guidelines above in your selection of any Auctioneer.

Be sure to book your Auctioneer early. Good Auctioneers can have their schedules start to fill more than a year in advance.

12.2   Order of live auction items

Consider these five guidelines when deciding on the order in which to auction off the live auction items:

1. Start with the least expensive item. You don't want to give people sticker shock right off the bat.
2. Older people tend to be the first ones to leave the event. So put items in the first half of the auction that appeal to older, retired people. For example, if you are selling a week-long vacation to Greece, chances are, it would appeal more to those who are retired and like to travel. Put artwork or antiques in the first half. A river rafting trip would appeal more to the younger crowd, so consider putting that kind of item in the second half of the live auction.

3. I like to put the most expensive items in the middle rather than at the end. There will be only one winning bidder. That means two or three other bidders will lose out and have money still left to spend. Give them an opportunity to spend it in the last half of the auction.
4. If you are selling a puppy (4.4), sell it in the first half of the live auction.
5. Fund-a-Program (12.23) should happen at or before the middle of the live auction, before anyone decides to leave.

Addendums

Live auction items can arrive right up to the day of the auction, after the printed programs have been printed. Some options would be:

- Put late items in the silent auction
- Save late items for next year's event
- Put late items in the live auction and advertise in an addendum to the printed program

An addendum is a sheet of paper listing the live auction items that come in after it is too late to include them in the printed program.

I like addendums for this reason: It is my opinion that people need time to think about buying an item. An addendum gives people a chance to read about last-minute-items.

I don't like addendums for these reasons: They easily fall out of printed programs and are usually printed small to allow multiple last-minute-items to fit on one page, which makes them hard to read. Addendums that are more than one page are awkward to handle. If you use an addendum consider these suggestions:

- Don't auction off your addendum items between the items in your printed program. You will confuse guests. Sell them after all the other auction items have been sold. You can give your guests a teaser by mentioning the addendum items during the live auction.
- Provide a sign that your Item Number Displayer (12.12) can display that says "**Addendum**".
- When designing and printing your addendum, follow the guidelines as explained in Design the Printed Program (9.1).

Sometimes new live auction items will present themselves in the middle of the live auction. At one auction I conducted, the celebrity Item Describer got caught up in the moment, took off her earrings and asked me to sell them. They went for a lot.

12.3   Display of live auction items

Here are some guidelines to consider when setting up and displaying live auction items:

- **Display all live auction items in one place**. Do not distribute them in various places within your event. Keep them together. Scattering live auction items make finding them confusing.
- **Identify the live auction items with a big sign** that says, "Live Auction". Without the sign, how are people going to know at a glance? It is best to eliminate any possible confusion.
- **Announce the location of the live auction items** periodically between the time guests arrive and the start of the live auction. Invite your guests to do a little "window shopping". The Silent Auction Emcee (11.1) can do this.

- **Number each item**. The number should correspond to the number of the live auction item in the printed program (9.1). Make sure the number is big enough and displayed so it is easily seen. If you are using PowerPoint to display a picture of the item on the big screen during the live auction, make sure the item number is on every slide.
- **Display items and their numbers in numeric order**. Items should also be displayed in the same order they are found in the printed program. This eliminates confusion.
- **Create a written description to display with each item**. The description should be written in a Times New Roman or Arial font, and the font size should be big enough to be easily read without having to bend over. The description should be the same as what is written in the printed program. See Design the Printed Program (9.1) for an example of what an alluring description should look like. If your item is a gift certificate, the written description you display should be displayed in its place.
- **Display something for each item**. If the actual item can be displayed, that is the best. If the item is a round of golf, display tees and golf balls. If the item includes eating at a restaurant, display a dinner place setting. If the item is a trip somewhere, display a poster from a travel agency. The way an item is packaged will make a difference in how much attention it gets. Use creative ways to draw people's attention. Display a picture of the product or service that will be auctioned off. With digital photography technology, it is relatively easy to take a picture and make a large print for display.
- **Move all the live auction items and displays to the stage area** shortly before the live auction begins, if needed, so the Item Displayer (12.13) will have easy access to them during the live auction.

- **Demonstrate the item if possible**. If you are selling a piano, guitar, or other musical instrument, find an expert and have them play something entertaining for the audience just before you auction it off. Give people an idea how they could sound if they bought this musical instrument.

I was at an event where a bicycle was going to be auctioned off. The bicycle was in a box, and required assembly. One of the organizers decided to dump everything out so everyone could get a glimpse of the actual bicycle parts. So here was the frame and seat and wheels and handlebars and nuts and bolts and gear assembly and a book of instructions in a pile on the floor. Now I know why bicycle advertisements don't show a pile of parts. It doesn't generate a desire to own that bike.

If you have something that requires assembly, either assemble it or leave it in the box. If you leave it in the box, try to display an attractive picture of the assembled item.

12.4   Sound system

A good sound system is critical for the live auction and is noted here so you will make sure a good one is used. Please refer Sound System (10.25) for important information about the sound system.

12.5   Stage and lighting

If the Auctioneer can see the potential bidders without a stage or raised platform, then it is not necessary to have one. If the audience is standing rather than sitting, then it is very helpful to the Auctioneer to be able to see over them – in which case, a stage or raised platform is good to have. For more information, refer to Stage Location and Setup (10.22)

Lighting in the room should be bright enough to allow the Auctioneer to see everyone adequately. A spotlight on the Auctioneer will cause the Auctioneer to see blackness where the audience is supposed to be. Please keep all spotlights off the Auctioneer. For more information, refer to Lighting (10.30).

12.6 Easels

Easels are useful when displaying signage, framed artwork, posters that represent live auction items such as vacation destinations, and Item Numbers (12.10).

12.7 Arrange to deliver large items

Arrange with the buyer, a good time to deliver a large item. Coordinate this with the Cashier (13.3) since it will be the Cashier that will receive payment and release the auction items to the winning bidders.

What if after selling a large item at the auction, the buyer cannot take delivery for a few days? In that case, you're going to need a place to store that item before you can deliver it. Coordinate post-event item storage needs with the Procurement Chair (4.9), who had to store auction items somewhere before the auction.

12.8 PowerPoint presentation of auction items

I've attended many auctions where a projector hooked up to a laptop computer projected pictures of live auction items onto a big screen as they were being described and sold. This might be a good idea for your auction.

If the item is a vacation, two or three slides of the destination can be shown. Eighteen holes of golf can be accompanied by a picture of the beautiful greens. For a dinner, a picture of the restaurant's interior or a cozy table for two might stir some interest.

Pictures can get people excited about an item or a service or an experience where a mere verbal description might not.

12.9   Arrange for live models and escorts

Arrange for live models to display jewelry and clothing that will be sold at the live auction. The models should roam among the guests during the social hour and at dinner time, telling people about the jewelry or clothing, and asking if they would like to try on what they are modeling.

Typically, people don't like to buy clothing or jewelry that they haven't had time to inspect. When people look at a model, they can get an idea of how they, themselves, would look wearing the jewelry or clothing. They also get a chance to try on the merchandise to get a feel for the fit and how they would look if they owned it.

You don't need to use expensive professional models. Find some volunteers that you feel would make good models at your event and train them. Don't assume they'll know what to do. Tell them *exactly* what you want them to do and then do some role playing. If professional models were to donate their services, take advantage of it.

Arrange for escorts to accompany people to the stage. Sometimes I auction off chefs. I have conducted entire chef auctions. People buy chefs for an evening to cook for small intimate groups or for large parties. In order to add a little show-biz to the live auction, I suggest that each chef be accompanied by an attractive, nicely dressed escort when they come up to the stage. Male chefs are to be escorted by females; female chefs are to be escorted by males.

Any person who is auctioned off should be escorted up to the stage. This might include celebrities or entertainers if they are going to come up to the stage before being auctioned off.

Sometimes I auction off dates with people. These bachelors and bachelorettes can be escorted, however, another good way to present them for auction is to have them come out from behind a curtain or from off-stage, by themselves, and walk the runway like a runway model would. A pre-auction rehearsal would be a good idea in this case. Invite a professional runway model to teach proper runway walking techniques.

12.10   Display of item numbers

Let's say there is a married couple in the audience who want to bid on item number 11. The auction begins and they pass the time talking to each other and to friends around them. When they want to know what item the Auctioneer is going to sell, they have to listen while the next item is being described. As they get caught up in conversation, item number 11 comes and goes without them being aware.

In order to keep that kind of scenario from happening, have big numbers printed or written on poster board or other material that can be displayed during the description and auctioning of each item.

For example, as item number one is being described, the Item Number Displayer (12.12) holds the number "1" high above her head and walks around the stage and into the audience. When the Auctioneer begins calling for bids, she puts the number on an easel for everyone to see whenever they look up at the stage.

When it's time for item number two, she parades a giant number "2" around and puts that number on the easel, replacing number one. Guests can find out at any time what item number the Auctioneer is selling simply by glancing up to the stage and seeing the number displayed on the easel.

12.11   Print Live Auction Bid Sheets

Prior to the event, you should print Live Auction Bid Sheets on two-part carbonless forms. Make one bid sheet for every live auction item. The Clerk fills in the Item Number, a short Description of the auction item, and the Fair Market

Value. The Fair Market Value is important for the winning bidder who wants to figure his or her purchase into this year's tax return.

The Auctioneer, upon selling the item, will say, "Sold for five hundred dollars to bidder number 79. Five hundred dollars. 79 the bidder." At that point, the Clerk fills in the amount and bid number, and gives the Live Auction Bid Sheet to the Runner (12.17). The Runner takes the Live Auction Bid Sheet to the Cashier who puts it in the winning bidder's file folder. Here is an example of a Live Auction Bid Sheet:

Homeless Foundation's 20xx Gala
Live Auction
Bid Sheet

Item Number:

Description:

Fair Market Value $

Amount Paid: $

Bid Number:

Buyer's Signature:

12.12   Assign Item Number Displayer

You will need to assign an Item Number Displayer if you are going to display Item Numbers (12.10) during the live auction. The Item Number Displayer holds up a large number to inform the audience which item is currently being auctioned off.

12.13   Assign Item Displayer

The Item Displayer adds to the entertainment factor of the live auction, as well as lets the audience see which item is going to be auctioned next. Here is what I expect from my Item Displayers:

1. I have nothing against men being Item Displayers, but I think women are more appealing to the general audience.
2. Display the item being described so that all bidders can see what they are going to be bidding on. Hold the item up and walk it around the stage, in front of the stage and through the audience. If the item is too large to carry, stand next to it with one hand on it, and the other hand pointing to it with the palm up.
3. Smile!
4. Often, toward the end of the bidding, there are two bidders bidding against each other. I tell my Item Displayers to take the item and put it in the lap of the person thinking about bidding again. When that person bids, take the item away and walk it over to the other bidder who is thinking about bidding again. This is fun for the audience to watch and motivates the bidders to keep the bidding going.

If the item is a gift certificate you still need to display something. This is where you get to be creative. And the more creative you are, the more fun the audience is going to have. Your display can take the form of theater. Consider the following examples:

- If your auction item is 18 holes of golf, have a couple of people come up on stage and do some mock-golfing.
- For a trip somewhere that has a beach, have some people dressed in beach attire set up their beach chairs on the stage and toss a beach ball to each other.
- If your auction item is a river rafting trip, have someone in a small raft paddle on the stage.

The idea is to do something to keep the audiences' attention. Make it entertaining. Remember, only a handful of people are going to bid on any particular item. Everyone else has to wait around. If they have something entertaining to watch, they'll be much happier when the item THEY are interested in comes up for bid. The more show-business you can put into your auction, the more entertaining it will be.

12.14   Assign Item Describer

I like to work with someone on stage with me who describes the items. I call this person the Item Describer. The Item Describer describes the item and I auction it off. This way, the audience sees two different faces and hears two different voices. It makes the live auction more interesting to watch.

Another reason I like working with an Item Describer is that when I'm calling for bids, the Item Describer has some time to prepare for the next item. When the Item Describer is describing the item, I can catch my breath and decide where I'm going to start the bidding on the next item. I can also decide if I want to add anything to the description I think would be of interest. Here is what I like every Item Describer to do:

1. Read the description of the next item to be auctioned. A description poorly read will put bidders to sleep. Therefore, it is important that you are familiar with every item before the live auction begins.
2. Make sure of correct pronunciations, especially names and places.
3. Speak clearly and look up at the audience as much as you can.
4. Speak into the microphone. Just because you can hear yourself doesn't mean everybody else can.
5. Paraphrase and put your own personality into the description. Show some enthusiasm.
6. Go easy on the alcohol. People dislike drunk Item Describers.
7. Be careful with humor – not to offend anyone.
8. Start by saying the item number so the bidders know where you are in the program. Say: "The next item is item number 10." or "Item number 10 is next". Describe the item, state its value, and end by telling who donated the item.
9. Be ready to describe the next item as soon as the Auctioneer finishes selling the last item. A long silent pause between items tends to result in the loss of momentum which causes the audience to get bored.

I have found that many TV news anchors and radio hosts make good Item Describers because they feel comfortable behind a microphone. Remember, you're looking for that entertainment value – someone with a good voice and a good sense of humor.

You may want to have more than one Item Describer. They can take turns describing the items and the audience gets to hear a variety of voices and see a variety of faces. It makes the auction more interesting.

A word of caution. A sports celebrity, although very famous and well-liked, doesn't always make a good Item Describer. There are no doubt exceptions to this rule, but keep it in mind.

The item describer should recognize the major sponsors and donors throughout the evening: "Before I describe the next item I just want to recognize the XYZ Corporation as a major sponsor of tonight's event. We have some representatives right over here. Thank you." Refer to Decide on Donor Incentives (1.15).

12.15   Prepare a script for Item Describer

The Item Describer (12.14) and the Auctioneer need to have the descriptions of the live auction items. The printed program may be used for this.

If the item descriptions contain names or places that are hard to pronounce, show somewhere on the page how to pronounce them correctly.

Make sure that whatever script the Item Describer uses is easy to read. An Item Describer I was once working with actually said to the audience, "Can this description be any harder to read?" It was written in a fancy font that was nearly impossible to decipher – it was the printed program.

If your Item Describer is a celebrity, in other words, a politician, an actor or actress, or a TV or radio personality, they will need a script to read. If they need to make announcements over the course of the event or introduce people to speak, write it all down for them. They can decide what parts to adlib and what parts to read.

12.16   Assign Bid Spotters

Do not underestimate the importance of your Bid Spotters. I have seen enough auctions to make this promise: The better your Bid Spotters, the more money you're going to make at your live auction and the more fun your guests are going to have. Bid Spotters are a very important element to the live auction. So put some thought into choosing people who will make good Bid Spotters. The best Bid Spotters are adults who are not afraid to yell in front of an audience.

Bid Spotters have one major responsibility: to be the Auctioneer's eyes. They will alert the Auctioneer to hands going up or nods or winks or whatever signs that guests may give indicating they are bidding.

How are they going to alert the Auctioneer? They are going to turn toward the Auctioneer, point to the person bidding, and yell to get the Auctioneer's attention. What are they going to yell? I suggest that Bid Spotters yell "Yup". Every bid needs a "Yup", whether the Auctioneer is looking at the bidder or not.

When hands are going up all over the place, there should be an abundance of "yupping" from the Bid Spotters. When the bidding slows down to just two people bidding against each other, there should be good loud "yups" when either party indicates they are bidding. If Bid Spotters do this with enthusiasm, they are good Bid Spotters.

Here's the exciting part about using good Bid Spotters. If they do their job as I have explained, guests will bid more often. That's a pretty bold statement. But I've seen it happen time and time again. Good Bid Spotters motivate people to bid.

Here is why I think that happens. When Bid Spotters point to a bidder and yell "Yup" in the Auctioneer's direction, it gives the bidder a small moment of recognition. It validates the bidder. And that small moment of attention gives the bidder a good feeling. It makes him or her feel important. People like to feel important. If you recall, making people feel important is the first objective in **The Four Objectives of a Successful Fundraiser.** When bidders feel this moment of recognition every time they bid, they tend to want to bid again. They bid, they get recognized, and they feel good. They bid again, they get recognized, and they feel good. But this only happens if the Bid Spotters are enthusiastic and point and yell every time someone bids.

I always try to arrange some time before the live auction begins to talk with my Bid Spotters. I gather them around me and tell them what I just explained. I emphasize the importance of yelling loudly. Then we have some fun practicing. We each yell "Yup" as loud as we can. I tell them over and over, "Point and yup. Be loud." I also explain, "You will be the entertainment tonight. You will make people feel good about bidding, and you will be entertaining to those who are not bidding."

I did an auction not too long ago in front of about 200 people. Before the auction began, I trained four ladies to be Bid Spotters. They said they were Bid Spotters the year before but never had to yell. I said, "I'll make you a promise. If you do what I just showed you, you will make more money, have happier guests, and have more fun than you did last year." They were psyched.

We did the auction. They yelled and pointed at every bidder. The auction was noisy with yups. What a great time we had. After the auction the Executive Director told me what a difference the yelling made. It was the most successful auction ever. My Bid Spotters felt a great sense of accomplishment as well.

When I train my Bid Spotters, I sometimes say, "Look. Almost everybody here is drinking. No matter how silly you might feel yelling in front of the audience tonight, tomorrow, no one will remember a thing – especially anything about the Bid Spotters." That usually gets a chuckle.

I also tell the Bid Spotters that I will introduce them to the audience at the beginning of the auction. So they need to be in their designated places when I am introduced. We don't want any of the guests to get startled when the Bid Spotter standing next to them starts yelling, "Yup yup yup."

I'll introduce the Bid Spotters by saying something like, "Standing around the room are people who are going to help me spot bids. We affectionately refer to them as Screamer-Yeller-Pointers. Screamer-Yeller-Pointers are your friends. Their sole purpose in life tonight is to help me recognize your bids. So they're going to be doing a lot of, well, screaming, yelling, and pointing. Screamer-Yeller-Pointers, wave to the audience so we know where you are. Okay, introductions have been properly made. Here's what's going to happen. So-and-so is going to introduce our items.

I'm going to auction them off. So without further ado, let's get started. So-and-so, tell us about item number one."

Where are the Bid Spotters supposed to stand? They should be scattered around the room evenly. Assign them an area but don't restrict them to that area. Tell them to go where the action is, but to always keep an eye on their designated area.

What if bids are being made all over the place and the Auctioneer is sure to see at least one of them? Should Bid Spotters still yell and point, even if the Auctioneer will probably accept a bid from somewhere else? The answer is yes. Every bid deserves a "Yup."

How many Bid Spotters are needed? I suggest one Bid Spotter for every 50 people. If Bid Spotters are in short supply, then recruit at least two: one for each side of the stage area.

Are there any other responsibilities assigned to Bid Spotters? Yes. If the Auctioneer does not know who the winning bidder is, the Bid Spotter should identify that person to the Auctioneer. If the Auctioneer cannot read the winning bidder's bid number, then a Bid Spotter can help communicate that number to the Auctioneer by yelling out the number or holding up fingers or both. Also, if you are going to send a Runner (12.17) to the winning bidder, the Bid Spotters can direct that Runner to where the winning bidder is sitting or standing.

I have seen Bid Spotters given a flag, sign, pompom, flashlight; something to wave to help get the Auctioneer's attention. I think it adds a bit of entertainment to the auction. Caution the Bid Spotters, however, to be careful not to accidentally whack a guest in the excitement of waving their attention-getters.

As a side-note, in the auction business, Bid Spotters are also known as "Ringmen". Ringmen are used at estate sales, auto auctions, livestock and other types of auctions for all the reasons mentioned above. An Auctioneer knows and appreciates the value of a good ringman.

Here is a summary of Bid Spotters' responsibilities:

1. Be in your assigned area when the Auctioneer introduces you.
2. When a guest bids, turn your head toward the Auctioneer, point to the bidder and yell, "Yup", loudly and with enthusiasm.
3. After the item is sold, identify the location of the successful bidder to the Auctioneer if necessary.
4. After the item is sold, make sure the successful bidder's number is quickly and accurately communicated to the Auctioneer. You might need to ask the successful bidder to hold up his or her bid number so it is visible to the Auctioneer. Or, you may decide it is better to yell out the bidder's number to the Auctioneer.
5. After the item is sold, identify the location of the successful bidder to the Runner (12.17) so the Runner can obtain necessary information.

12.17 Assign Runners

Runners are responsible for getting signatures on the Live Auction Bid Sheets (12.11) from successful bidders. They will be stationed in a centralized location near the Clerk. A rotation will be set up so that one Runner is always available.

Each time an item is sold, the next Runner in line will take the Live Auction Bid Sheet on a clipboard from the Clerk to the successful bidder to get a signature (12.29).

Bid Spotters will help Runners find the right people but Runners still need to pay close attention to see where the successful bidders are sitting or standing.

Runners will leave a copy of the signed winning bid sheet with each successful bidder. They may also be asked to present a gift to each successful bidder, such as a long-stemmed rose (12.20).

If a successful bidder feels an error has been made and declines to sign a winning bid sheet, The Runner should inform someone who has the authority to resolve the problem – like the Auction Chair.

After obtaining a signature from the successful bidder, the Runner will take the Live Auction Bid Sheet to the Cashier, then return to the clerk and wait for his or her next turn.

Runners may be asked to take the Live Auction Bid Sheet directly to the Cashier without visiting the winning bidder. The Live Auction Bid Sheet contains the following:

- Item number
- Description of item or service
- Fair market value
- Amount paid
- Bid number
- Buyer's signature

All but the signature should be filled in when Runners get the Live Auction Bid Sheet from the Clerk.

12.18   Assign a Clerk

The Clerk is responsible for filling out the Live Auction Bid Sheets (12.11). Before the live auction begins, the Clerk should write in the item number, a brief description of the item or service, and the fair market value. Then, when the item is declared sold by the Auctioneer, the Clerk records the winning amount and the winning bid number.

The Clerk should sit near the Auctioneer and pay close attention when the Auctioneer calls out the winning amount and winning bid number. If the Clerk is not sure about the bidder's number or amount, he or she should interrupt the Auctioneer *immediately* and ask for it. "Hey, what was that amount?" or "What was that bid number"?

The Clerk will put the filled-out Live Auction Bid Sheet on a clipboard and give to the next Runner (12.17) in line.

12.19   Live auction step-by-step

The forth objective in the **Four Objectives of a Successful Fundraiser** is to get guests caught up in the thrill of bidding. We do this by putting show-business into the live auction. We use show-biz to keep the audience entertained. We want to entertain the bidders to keep them bidding and the non-bidders to keep them sitting. Guests are going to be spending a lot of time at their tables. The more entertaining and fun and interesting you can make it, the less likely your guests will leave early.

As a Live Auction Chair, you are a theatrical producer. Your live auction should be a show, put on by entertainers. The Auctioneer is the star of the show and is supported by his or her co-stars. They would include the Item Describer, the Bid Spotters, the Item Displayers, and the Item Number Displayer. Here is an example of a live auction agenda. When it's time for the live auction to start:

1. The emcee introduces the **Item Describer**.
2. The Item Describer introduces the **Auctioneer**.
3. The **Auctioneer** does a short introduction, asks people to bid by raising their bid cards, introduces the **Bid Spotters** who are already in their assigned places, and then asks the **Item Describer** to describe item number one.
4. The **Item Describer** describes the item.
5. While the item is being described, the **Item Displayer** displays the item. The item might also be displayed on a jumbo screen for all to see. The **Item Displayer** might also dress in a silly costume that relates to the item or service up for auction. Short skits could be enacted around an item or service by a cast of players.
6. While the item is being described, the **Item Number Displayer** walks around, displaying a poster that has the current item number on it.
7. The **Auctioneer** starts to auction off the item.

8. The Item **Number Displayer** puts the item number on an easel for guests to see.

9. As people raise their bid cards to bid, the **Bid Spotters** identify the bidders by pointing to the bidders and yelling "YUP!"

10. The **Auctioneer** sells the item to the highest bidder and announces the winner's bid number and amount.

11. The **Clerk** records the winning bid number and amount on the Live Auction Bid Sheet.

12. The **Runner** takes the Live Auction Bid Sheet from the **Clerk** and does one of two things:

    1. The Runner takes the bid sheet to the Cashier, and returns to the Clerk and waits for the next bid sheet.

    2. The Runner takes the bid sheet to the winning bidder, for a signature. The Runner also takes a small gift to the winning bidder like a long-stem rose (12.20). Then the Runner takes the signed bid sheet to the Cashier, and returns to the Clerk and waits for the next bid sheet. The purpose of the gift is to make the winning bidder feel pampered.

13. Repeat numbers 4 through 12 until all the items are sold.

Keep Track of the Second Highest Bidder

Imagine a winning bidder purchasing a vacation package and then deciding that maybe it wasn't such a good idea after all. The bidder approaches you and says, "You're really going to hate me, but I shouldn't have bought this trip, and so I'm returning it. Sorry."

What do you do now? You can't put the item back in the auction because the auction is over. If only you knew who the second highest bidder was so you could offer it to that person for the last price at which he or she bid. You can only do that if you keep track of the second highest bidders.

Even if you only knew at what table number the second highest bidder was sitting, you could contact all the couples who were assigned to sit at that table and ask if they were interested in purchasing the item for the second highest bid.

The point is, it might be worth the extra effort to record the second highest bidder's name, bid number, or table number in case the winning bidder comes down with buyer's remorse. Also record the second highest bid amount.

Treat the Audience to an Unexpected Treat

Surprise the audience with an unexpected treat. Little surprises make sitting through the live auction more fun. Consider delivering treats to each guest every 20 minutes or half hour of the auction. Try some sort of snack in mini-bags. Buy mixed nuts by the volume and put them in bowls for tables or in individual paper cups for each guest. Cookies make a nice treat. Consider sample shampoo, perfume, lotion or facial soap as treats. How about champagne, long stemmed red roses, glow-sticks, candy bars, cheese and cracker plates, hot coffee, Crackerjack, finger sandwiches, or veggies and dip?

No Breaks

Please say the following out loud: "There will be no breaks in the live auction." This is important. Breaks tend to cause an auction to lose momentum. It's hard to get people back into the bidding mood, and it's hard to get people back to the auction stage if they have wandered off.

No singers, dancers or other entertainment between auction items. No breaking for dinner, stopping for desert, or halting for a last chance to bid on silent auction items. There are two possible exceptions to this rule: (1) to have an occasional drawing, and (2) to make an emotional appeal before the Fund-a-Program (12.23). Other than that, when you start a live auction, you should keep it going until the last item has been sold. Otherwise you stand to lose momentum.

12.20 Gifts for successful bidders

In Live Auction Step-by-step (12.19), one of the suggestions was to give a small gift to each winning bidder. It was also suggested that a long-stem rose works well. If you decide to do this, you will need to get enough gifts – one gift for every live auction item to be sold.

If you decide to use a long-stem rose or any type of flower as a gift, be sure that each stem is in its own clear plastic "water tube" that commonly comes with single roses. Otherwise the flowers will wilt and guests will try to preserve their flowers by sticking them in their ice water. But ultimately, the flowers won't last very long.

Reward Everyone at the Winning Bidder's Table

Picture this. The bidding has been going back and forth between numerous bidders. Finally, it appears one last bidder remains. "Sold!" says the Auctioneer. The audience applauds. The winning couple hug, and a mini-celebration ensues. Before the excitement dies down at their table, someone comes up to the winning bidder and displays a bottle of champagne. As that is taking place, another person places champagne glasses in front of each guest at the table and the server pours the champagne. Everyone at the table gets rewarded because the winning bidder was at their table.

Look what this accomplishes. Everyone at the table shares in the celebration. The winning bidder gets patted on the back by everyone at the table for making the reward possible. Being the winning bidder felt good, but being the object of everyone's praise makes it all the sweeter. After the drinks are poured, the glasses are raised and the winning bidder is toasted.

212

Now look what else happens. Guests at surrounding tables take notice. For the rest of the live auction, when anyone bids, everyone at their table encourages them to bid again. Bidders not only bid to win the item or service being auctioned, but to become the honored provider of the coveted table reward.

In order to make this happen, you need to do some advance preparation:

- You'll need to estimate how many bottles of champagne will be needed.
- You'll need to make sure there are enough champagne glasses to go around. Use nice crystal or elegant looking plastic champagne glasses.
- Assign two volunteers to make the presentation after each live auction item is sold.
- Make the presentation as quickly as possible.
- Substitute wine in place of champagne if so desired, along with the appropriate glasses.
- Have a bottle of non-alcoholic beverage on hand for non-drinkers.
- Make a subtle announcement at the beginning of the live auction that champagne will be served to the entire table of each winning bidder.

This is a good way to pamper (by the table) and get people caught up in the thrill of bidding.

12.21   Meet with the Auctioneer

If you've done your homework, you have chosen an Auctioneer that you have seen perform at another fundraiser, or one that has been highly recommended by someone who has seen him or her perform (12.1). I suggest that you do not assume the Auctioneer can read your mind and do what you expect. I think it's a good idea to meet with the Auctioneer a week or two before the auction to set some expectations. Consider the following topics for discussion:

- **Arrival time**. What time should the Auctioneer arrive at the event?
- **Meeting place**. Determine the location where you and the Auctioneer are to meet.
- **Dress code**. It's my opinion the Auctioneer should be dressed a step above the guests. If the event is a black tie affair, male Auctioneers should wear a tuxedo and female Auctioneers should dress in evening wear or an elegant suit.
- **The agenda**. Go over what time various events are supposed to begin, particularly, what time the Auctioneer should expect to perform.
- **Volunteer coordination meeting**. Decide the best time and location for the Auctioneer to meet with the volunteers. I make it a point to talk with all the live auction volunteers, namely:
  - o the Item Number Displayer (12.12)
  - o the Item Displayers (12.13)
  - o the Item Describer (12.14)
  - o the Bid Spotters (12.16)
  - o the Runners (12.17)
  - o and the Clerk (12.18)
  - o This usually happens a few minutes before the guests arrive on the day of the event. The purpose of this little training meeting is to make sure everyone knows what they are supposed to do.
- **Can the Auctioneer bring a guest?** Let the Auctioneer know whether or not a guest can come for free.
- **Is the Auctioneer invited to eat with guests?** If so, the Auctioneer's name should be included on the guest list at the registration table.

- **Provide an early list of auction items**. It would be beneficial if the Auctioneer had a "rough draft" of the live auction items a few days before the auction to become familiar with them. The Auctioneer most likely will not need to see the finalized list until the night of the event.
- **Provide retail values**. It is helpful to the Auctioneer to know the estimated retail value of each of the items. Then he or she will have a better idea where to start the bidding and how far to push it. If you are tempted to inflate the estimated value of items, don't. Some of your guests will have an idea what the items are worth, and perhaps know where they can buy them on discount. Don't try to trick them into thinking the items are worth more. They might feel you consider them to be uninformed.
- **Payment arrangements**. Should the Auctioneer submit an invoice? Should the Auctioneer expect payment before, the night of, or after the event?

Following are some other topics you may want to discuss with the Auctioneer:

Consignment Items

When someone consigns an item to you to sell at the live auction, the consignor requires a payment for that item after it sells. The payment may be what the consignor paid wholesale for the item (or maybe a little more). So you need to get at least the consignor's portion of the money out of the item or you lose money.

Let's say you have an item on the live auction with a consignment value of $500.00. Do you start the bidding at $500.00? Or, do you start below $500.00 and hope someone bids up to and past $500.00? And if you don't get a $500.00 bid, what do you do, confess there is a minimum bid? I like to start the bidding a little higher than the consignor's portion so if you only get one bid, you make some money rather than just break even. I'll tell everyone that the minimum starting bid is $600.00 and start the bidding there. If nobody bids, I'll skip over that item and go onto the next one. Then at the end of the auction, I'll say, "Ladies and gentlemen, I've just been given authorization to lower the starting bid on this item to $500.00", or whatever the prearranged amount is. There has hardly been a time when I haven't sold everything in the live auction with minimum starting bids.

As a last resort, it may be easier to sell an item and break even than have to return the item to the consignor.

Make sure the Auctioneer knows which items have minimum starting bids. Then have a predetermined plan for your Auctioneer to follow if you don't get the minimum bid.

Jewelry and Clothing

Jewelry and clothing should be displayed by models (12.9) from the time guests begin to enter the event. People rarely purchase jewelry or clothing unless they have had a chance to see it up close and even try it on. So, before I start the bidding, I ask if there is anyone who would like to see this item up close. I'll usually get a hand or two. At that point I'll say, "I'll tell you what let's do. For those of you who want to see this necklace up close, please wave our model over so you can take a closer look. Right now, let's move onto the next item and after we've sold that one, we'll come back to auction off this beautiful necklace."

This way, guests who weren't interested in the merchandise earlier who have changed their minds, can examine the jewelry or clothing up close, which may result in them wanting to bid.

Two of the Same Item

If you have two of the same items to sell, rather than put one up for bid and sell it and then put the other one up for bid and sell it, just sell the two items to the two highest bidders. It will save time.

I'll ask the second highest bidder if he or she will buy the item for the same amount as the winning bidder. If they say "no" then I'll ask if they'd be willing to purchase it at their last highest bid. If they say "yes" then I usually reduce the highest buyer's bid to that amount so the highest bidder doesn't go away mad.

Introduction of Bid Spotters

The Auctioneer should announce to your audience at the beginning of the auction that there are Bid Spotters (12.16) standing within the audience, and that they will be yelling to make the Auctioneer aware of people bidding. This will give people fair warning that the person standing next to them might all of a sudden start yelling.

12.22   Delivery of large live auction items

Some items may be too large for the successful bidder to carry home. Arrange for large items to be delivered at no cost. Be sure to announce that large items will be delivered for free at the beginning of the live auction. This task takes away the excuse, "But honey, how would we get it home?"

Coordinate with the Cashier Chairperson (13.3) who will be receiving payments and making delivery arrangements with the winning bidders. Have a form at checkout to get names, addresses, phone numbers, date and time of delivery, item number and description of the item.

12.23   Fund-a-Program

Fund-a-Program is one of the most powerful, money-making strategies I've come across – if it's done right. The only things people get for their donation are 1) a few seconds of recognition, 2) a good feeling knowing their donation will help your cause, and 3) a tax deduction. They don't take anything home with them like they would if they bought a regular auction item. When they raise their hands to donate, it is because of how they feel at the moment. So what makes them want to donate?

Fund-a-Program is driven by emotion. That's why it is so important to focus on achieving **The Four Objectives of a Successful Fundraiser** before you launch into the Fund-a-Program. When your guests 1) feel important, 2) gain a desire to support your cause, 3) want what you're selling (in this case a chance to help fund your program), and 4) get caught up in the excitement of the live auction – whether they've bid or not – they will feel more generous during your Fund-a-Program.

Here's how the Fund-a-Program works. The Auctioneer says, "Ladies and gentlemen, you'll notice in your printed program that the next item is called Fund-a-Program. Fund-a-Program is a way we raise money for a particular program in need. In a moment, I'm going to ask each one of you to donate a certain amount of money. But in order for you to feel inspired to donate, you need to know where your money is going. Here to inspire you, is our Executive Director. Please welcome to the stage, Mary Smith."

Mary Smith takes the microphone and in one or two minutes tells how desperately the school needs new computer software. Her prepared speech evokes emotion as she explains how new software will give students the advantage in a technologically driven world; and how without new software, students, even YOUR children, will fall behind other students in other schools who have the latest software at their disposal. "We just cannot let that happen in a competitive society," she says.

Mary leaves the stage to the audience's applause. The Auctioneer says, "Thank you Mary. Now you get a chance to feel the satisfaction of knowing that you made a difference in the lives of our students. We invite you to come see the new software you helped to purchase and how it will be helping the students."

218

"So, here goes. What happens now is up to you. Our fingers are crossed and we're holding our breath. I'm going to start with an amount and then drop to a smaller amount and continue to do that until you've all had a chance to help us out. Those of you, who can dig deep into your pockets and come up with $5,000 for our computer software program, please raise your bid cards now."

Silence. I've seen it get deadly quiet during this moment. If no one raises their bid card after 10 seconds, and if it is really quiet, I'll say, "This is typically the quietest time of the evening", and I'll get a few chuckles.

"OK, let's take it down to a more comfortable level. $2,500", says the Auctioneer. Silence.

"All right, who can help us out with a $1,000 donation?" A bid card goes up. "Number 150. Thank you very much! Yes, applause is good!" Another bid card goes up. "Number 80. Thank you, sir! That's what I'm talkin about." Another 10 second wait.

"Let's drop it down to $500" More bid cards go up. "Number 45, thank you. Number 205, thank you. Number 71, thank you," and so on until all the numbers have been read and the donors thanked. The Auctioneer must make sure to say "thank you" to each donor to show appreciation and to give the Clerk enough time to record the numbers.

"Ok, let's make it easy. $100." Bid cards go up, the Auctioneer calls out the numbers and thanks each donor.

"All right, this is the last time. I want to see everybody's bid card who hasn't raised it. 50 dollars. You can scrounge up 50 bucks, and every bit helps." Bid cards go up, numbers are read, and donors thanked until all bid cards have been recognized. The Auctioneer then makes one last attempt by saying, "For some of us 50 dollars is a lot of money and requires a sacrifice. Take a good feeling home with you. Last call for fifty dollars." Two more hands go up and are recognized.

"Ladies and gentlemen, thank you for your generosity. Give yourselves a nice big round of applause.

As soon as the total amount has been tallied, the Auctioneer or the Item Describer says, "Ladies and gentlemen. Do you want to know what the final tally for our Fund-a-Program is? Thanks to your generosity, we raised six thousand…four hundred…and fifty dollars!" Applause erupts, confetti falls from the rafters, the band strikes up a lively tune, high-fives are exchanged among guests, there is dancing in the aisles… Can you tell I like Fund-a-Program?

The first time I experimented with Fund-a-Program, there was a guest attending the fundraiser who read in his printed program, that a Fund-a-Program was scheduled to occur during the live auction. He hunted down the Executive Director and pledged to match every dollar collected during Fund-a-Program up to $25,000. It took us about ten minutes to raise $25,000 and with the $25,000 match, we raised $50,000. Not bad for one little strategy.

At another fundraiser, the Executive Director pulled me aside in the middle of the live auction, while an auction item was being described and said, "Let's do fund-an-item next." I said, "Are you sure? We haven't planned this at all." He said, "Yeah, let's do it." I said, "OK, will you give an emotional appeal?" He said, "I will."

After I auctioned off the next item I said, "Ladies and gentlemen, the next item isn't in your program, but at this time, we would like to do what we call Fund-An-Item." I explained what it was, the Executive Director gave an eloquent emotional appeal and we raised $7,500. The audience was emotionally ready for it. **The Four Objectives of a Successful Fundraiser** had been achieved. That's why it worked.

Here are some guidelines to make Fund-a-Program work for you:

- Call it Fund-a-Program, Fund-an-Item, Fund-a-Project, Fund-a-Future, Fund-a-Whatever.
- Put details about Fund-a-Program in the printed program so people can read about it.

- If possible, take pictures of the item in need, or items needing replacing and show on the big screen for all to see.
- Fund-a-Program should take place at or before the middle of the live auction before anybody leaves.
- All guests need bid numbers, displayed big enough to be read from the stage area.
- Focus on achieving **The Four Objectives of a Successful Fundraiser** before you launch into the Fund-a-Program.
- Warn the Clerk, in advance, to be ready to write down bid numbers fast.
- Tell the Bid Spotters, before the auction, to alert the Auctioneer of any hands that go up that the Auctioneer does not see.
- Recruit someone to total the amount raised for later announcement.
- Keep the emotional appeal short. Tell where the money will go, and why. You want to leave your guests with misty eyes when the emotional appeal is over.
- A wireless microphone will allow the Auctioneer to roam through the audience to read bid numbers.
- Remind the Auctioneer to thank each donor after reading their bid number. It gives the Clerk time to record the bid numbers and it gives each donor a few seconds of well deserved recognition and appreciation.
- Starting with a $5,000 request gets sticker-shock out of the way and makes any lower amounts feel better. And who knows, you may get a donor. I've been pleasantly surprised many times.
- Announce the total amount raised later in the program.
- Ask a corporation, bank, insurance company, or a rich philanthropist to match donations up to a certain

amount. Use your matching dollars as an incentive to get your guests to donate.

- Make Fund-a-Program an annual tradition.
- Fund-a-Program does not work as well if the audience is rowdy, noisy, scattered, or standing up.

Two Other Incentives for Fund-a-Program

There are two other incentives that I have used to motivate people to donate to Fund-a-Program. They are:

1. A certificate of appreciation
2. A chance to win something in a drawing

The Auctioneer says, "As an incentive, everyone who raises their hand will get a Certificate of Appreciation like this one (holds one up) showing our gratitude for your support, suitable for hanging in your office, with the intent that after a few years of supporting Fund-a-Program, you will have a bunch of these hanging on your wall showing all your customers and clients that you are a major supporter of the community. And who wouldn't want to do business with a major supporter of the community?"

"As a second incentive, everyone who raises their hand will have a ticket with their bid number on it placed in a bowl, and a drawing will immediately follow the Fund-a-Program."

After all the requests for donations have been made, the Auctioneer says, "Ladies and gentlemen, thank you for your generosity. Tonight you have really made a difference for Such-and-Such a cause. Give yourselves a nice big round of applause. Shall we have the drawing?" The drawing is held and the prizes are awarded. Here are some guidelines to make these two incentives work:

- Recruit someone to write bid numbers on tickets for the drawing.

- Remember to bring tickets, a pen, and a bowl for the drawing.
- Procure some terrific prizes for the drawing. Three or four prizes will give your donors a greater chance to win, and thus, more incentive to donate. You should announce the prizes in the printed program and during the introduction of Fund-a-Program.
- Conduct the drawing directly after Fund-a-Program.
- If you use the Certificate of Appreciation as an incentive, show an example of one to the audience, or project an example of one on a screen for all to see. Make sure to send a certificate to each donor soon after the event.

Certificates of Appreciation

Certificates of Appreciation are pretty easy to make. Go to an office supply store and buy blank certificates. Then, with your word processor, create the wording you feel is appropriate and run the certificates through the printer.

For a list of companies that provide blank certificates, go to: **www.LetsDoAnAuction.com/resources.htm.**

Following, is an example of a Certificate of Appreciation.

12.24 Selling sponsorships

I have sold sponsorships to build latrines in third-world countries. I've sold sponsorships to build small hospitals, schools, greenhouses, wells, and brick stoves. I've sold sponsorships to hire teachers, provide scholarships, purchase library books, and pay for computer equipment.

Selling sponsorships is like doing a Fund-a-Program (12.23) multiple times during the live auction. People pledge a specific amount of money that will pay for a particular item or project. For example, you might sell sponsorships for $250 each to provide disabled children opportunities to attend summer camp for 2 weeks. You might sell sponsorships for $25 each to provide a winter cap, a pair of mittens and boots to children in need.

You can mix the auction items with the sponsorships. Sell an item, then a sponsorship, then another item, then another sponsorship. To make this work, focus on achieving

The Four Objectives of a Successful Fundraiser before you begin selling sponsorships, and make a short emotional appeal while describing each sponsorship.

As an incentive you can offer a certificate of appreciation to each sponsor as explained in Fund-a-Program (12.23). But on this certificate, include a picture of the item the sponsor donated money to buy, or the structure the sponsor donated money to build. That's a certificate the sponsor will be proud to show off. Another incentive is to use a drawing as explained in Fund-a-Program.

12.25   Asking for donations of "time"

I was conducting the auction for an organization that helped troubled youth. We sold sponsorships (12.24) to fund various programs mixed in with some great auction items. Then we did something different. Instead of asking guests to donate their money, we asked them to donate their time. "Those of you, who can spend two hours of your time as a tutor or to teach a skill, sometime over the next year, please raise your bid card now." Hands went up all over the place.

Look what donating time accomplishes. Obviously, it benefits those receiving the help. But there is another equally important benefit. The people donating their time get to experience, first hand, what the organization is all about by becoming personally involved. They will feel the satisfaction that can only be felt by serving. Often, when people become personally involved, their desire to support the organization increases. When that happens they are apt to agree to be on a committee, or invite their friends to the next fundraiser, or spend more money at the next fundraiser. Here are some things that will help make this strategy more effective:

- **Give an emotional appeal.** Do a short emotional appeal as explained in Fund-a-Program (12.23), to let guests know how their time will be used and how important you feel their two hours of service will be.

225

- **Thank each donor.** When people raise their bid cards to donate time, make sure the Auctioneer reads the number on each bid card as explained in Fund-a program and thanks each donor. The Clerk (12.18) records the bid numbers as the Auctioneer calls them out. You are going to build a relationship with these people.
- **Get donor information.** Make sure you get a phone number and an email address from each donor. That way, you can notify all the donors of available opportunities to serve over the course of the next year by email. Or, you can call them from time to time to tell them how needed they are.
- **Send a thank-you note.** Soon after the auction, send each donor a hand-written card, thanking them for agreeing to donate their time and how you are looking forward to their help in the near future. They need to feel that the time they promised to donate is a big deal.
- **Call with available opportunities.** Send an occasional email to those who have promised to donate time and ask for help. If you get no response, call them. It's harder to turn down a personal phone call than it is to ignore an email.
- **Invite donors back.** After people have donated their two hours of time, as they are leaving, ask them if they would be interested in coming back to donate two more hours. If they say "Yes", then you can continue building a relationship with them. If they say, "I'll think about it," ask if you can continue to send emails about available opportunities.
- **Send a thank-you note after the donation is complete.** Send a hand-written note thanking each person who donated their time. Expressing gratitude is an important part in building relationships.
- **Advertise in your newsletter.** If you send out a newsletter, advertise opportunities for people to help.

13. Cashiers Chair

13.1 Cashier location and setup

The Cashier table should be set up in a conspicuous location, but out of the way of the main stream of traffic. Consider placing a sign overhead that reads "Cashier".

You need to have enough Cashiers on hand to avoid guests having to stand in line for very long. If guests get upset about standing in line, they may leave with an unpaid bill, forcing you to track them down in the days or weeks following your event. You only have to do that once to learn that it is easier to provide more Cashiers than to collect accounts receivable.

Plan on having enough electrical outlets and extension cords for the computers and credit card terminals you'll be using.

13.2 Train the Cashiers

A smooth cashiering system is the result of good training. Be sure your Cashiers are well trained. As the Cashier Chairperson, you become the designated trouble-shooter to resolve any questions or problems that might arise during the cashiering process during the event.

Train and use as many Cashiers as you feel necessary to keep the lines moving. You will also need to train the volunteers you will use to retrieve items for winning bidders to take home.

13.3 The cashiering and checkout process

Set up a simple filing system by providing a file folder for each bid number. If you issue 300 bid numbers then you will have 300 file folders. This is something you can reuse every year.

File Silent Auction Bid Sheets

After the silent auction closes, or a section of the silent auction closes, a volunteer assigned to the silent auction will bring you the bid sheets. You will get one part of a two-part Silent Auction Bid Sheet for each silent auction item sold. The winning bid number and amount will be on each bid sheet. You will file the bid sheet in the appropriate bidder's file folder according to bid number.

The second part of these two-part bid sheets will be delivered to the winning bidders by someone on the Silent Auction Committee (11.9).

File Live Auction Bid Sheets

During the live auction, a Runner (12.17) will deliver to you, one part of a two-part Live Auction Bid Sheet for each live auction item sold. The winning bid number and amount will be on each bid sheet you receive. You will file the bid sheet in the appropriate bidder's file folder according to bid number.

The second part of this two-part bid sheet will be given to each winning bidder as a receipt by the Runner.

Have a Guest Spreadsheet Handy

Make sure all of your Cashiers have access to a Registration Spreadsheet (8.6) in case someone comes to checkout and doesn't know their bid number. The spreadsheet will be sorted by guest name and show each guest's assigned bid number. Since your files will be sorted by bid number, you will need to know the bid number of each guest who comes to the Cashier table.

Checkout

When a guest comes to the Cashier table to pay for his or her items, the Cashier says, "What is your bidding number?"

"155", says the guest.

The Cashier gets folder number 155, and pulls out any Silent Auction Bid Sheets and Live Auction Bid Sheets.

"Well, you have one silent auction item and one live auction item, says the Cashier, "The total comes to $1,550. How do you want to pay for that?"

The Cashier collects the money in the form of check, cash or credit card. If the Cashier receives a check, he or she writes the bid number on the check.

Now your winning bidder needs to take possession of the item(s) or certificate(s) he or she has just paid for. Consider the following two ways to accomplish this:

- As the winning bidder is paying for his or her items, give the bidder's bid sheet(s) to a volunteer who will quickly retrieve the items for the winning bidder. The closer the items are to the Cashier area, the easier the retrieval process will be. Have the winning bidder initial the receipts that you keep, indicating he or she has taken possession.

- With a rubber stamp, stamp "Paid" on the winning bidder's bid sheets. The winning bidder then goes to where the silent and live auction items are being kept, presents the stamped receipts to a volunteer who helps the winning bidder find his or her items to take home.

There may be items that are too large for the buyer to carry home. In that case, delivery arrangements should be made (12.7). Arrange with the buyer, a time when someone will be available to receive the item. Then communicate this information to the Auction Chair who will be in charge of making deliveries.

13.4   Arrange for computer setup

If you plan to use computers at the Cashier table, be sure of the following well in advance of the event start time:

- Your software works as expected
- Your printer works and will print receipts – fast enough – and you have plenty of paper
- Electrical outlets are conveniently located and there are enough of them
- You have the necessary extension cords
- There is enough duct tape to cover all the extension cords where people walk

13.5   Arrange for a "paper" backup system

Arrange for a "paper" backup system in case the computer system fails. I probably wouldn't have thought to bring this up if I had not actually seen computer systems fail at fundraisers. I've seen printers fail to work so receipts could not be printed.

I was at one auction where the electricity in the entire hotel went out. The guests had just received their dinner and the only light to be had was from a single decorative candle on each of the tables. The hotel audio/visual man, fortunately, was able to plug the sound system into the auxiliary electricity powered by a generator allowing the sound system to work. But there were no lights.

The big question was, how were we going to conduct the live auction when we couldn't see the guests? A lot of money was riding on the live auction and if we couldn't hold it, the fundraiser would be a fund-loser.

I had a big flashlight in my car, and a volunteer was able to find another one for me. I told the Event Chairperson, "The auction will go on."

I arranged for a volunteer to shine my flashlight on me while I was up on stage. The Item describer used the other flashlight to read the item descriptions. I asked that people bid by raising the candle on their table. It was a very interesting auction. I called for bids, and candles went up and down throughout the audience. We sold all the live auction items. The evening turned out to be a memorable experience for everyone there.

It could have been a disaster. But we were prepared – and lucky. The Cashiers threw together a paper checkout system, procured more flashlights, and checkout proceeded as best it could under the circumstances.

Perhaps you'll never need a "paper" backup system. But it wouldn't hurt to be prepared. Suggest to your volunteers to carry a flashlight in their cars with fresh batteries – just in case.

13.6   Handle the Cash

Be prepared to handle cash. Whether you use a strong box or a shoe box, keep it out of site when not using it, and never leave it unattended. When you are using your money box, make it hard for someone to snatch it and run.

13.7   Credit card setup

I tell Event Chairs that they are leaving money on the table if they don't accept credit cards. In this day and age, credit cards are a way of life. People don't carry cash and checks so much anymore. But they do carry credit cards.

There will be people who come to your event with no intention of buying anything. Other people will come having set a limit on what they intend to spend. These same people may change their mind and decided to buy something, but only have a credit card with which to pay. If you don't accept credit cards, you eliminate these people from bidding.

If you have a merchant account you can use the manual "knuckle-busters" to record credit card payments. If you use credit card terminals, you can swipe guests' credit cards when they check out. You'll have to be able to connect to a telephone line in the case of terminals. If you have more than one credit card terminal, you'll need multiple telephone lines. If you only use one credit card terminal, it could slow down the checkout process.

There are some companies that provide credit card terminals to be used at your fundraiser. The terminals store credit card information you collect from your guests. Then later, you "upload" the data over the phone to the company from which you borrowed the terminals. They process all the credit card numbers, keep a small percentage of the proceeds, and electronically transfer the remaining funds to your bank account.

For a list of companies that provide credit card terminals for fundraising events, go to **www.LetsDoAnAuction.com/resources.htm**.

13.8   Arrange to check buyers' receipts

Assign volunteers to check buyer's receipts before they leave with their items. I've attended events where winning bidders were allowed to pick up their own items. I would see them standing in the Cashier line with items in hand. In a situation like this it wouldn't be hard for someone to accidentally take home the wrong items, or more items than they should.

Assign volunteers to stand at the exits and compare the winning bidders' receipts with the items they allegedly bought. Have a plan in place to handle the situation when someone's receipt doesn't match what they're carrying, and when someone cannot find the item that he or she won – and paid for.

14. Thank-You-Letter Chair

14.1 Thank all contributors

Do not skip this step. This step is so important in continuing relationships, that I have created a Thank-You-Letter Chair to make sure it happens. Within 30 days of your event, you should thank everyone who donated time, services, money or items. The bigger the donation, the more personalized the thank-you should be. Let me suggest five "thank-you" levels.

1. **A visit**. This is the ultimate going-out-of-your-way to say thank you. Think how your visit would be received; what an impression you would make.
2. **A telephone call and a hand-written note**. This should go out from the Event Chairperson to your biggest bidders, your biggest donors, your chairpersons and your hardest working volunteers. "I just wanted to thank you for your sacrifice and hard work. You have no idea how important your help was to us." The address on the envelope should be hand-written.
3. **A hand-written note**. This should go out to those who contributed time, money or items on a more modest level. "I just want to thank you for your attendance and your generous donation." The address on the envelope should be hand-written.
4. **Form letters addressing the recipients by name**. These are mass thank-you notes or postcards sent to everyone else who donated or attended. Form letters will not make a lasting impression on the recipients – unless – there is a personal hand-written note at the bottom. "John and Mary, thank you for coming and supporting us." Then signed. The address on the envelope should be hand-written.

5. **Form letters and mailing labels.** This is your most impersonal method of thanking people: a form letter stuffed in an envelope with a computer-generated address label. This is the fastest way of getting thank you letters out. But what kind of message does it really send? When YOU receive a letter like this, what is your reaction? I suggest these kinds of letters are counter-productive. Rather than making recipients feel validated and important, they could discourage people from getting involved with your event again. After all, they did buy a ticket to get in.

The more personalized the thank-you, the better. Imagine if everyone received a card with a short hand-written note. Would it have a significant long-range effect?

Here's an idea worth considering. Have the beneficiaries of your organization (especially if they are children) write thank-you notes. These sorts of notes might even get displayed on some recipients' refrigerator doors.

Coordinate your efforts with the following chairpersons who should be maintaining lists of people who should receive a thank-you.

- Volunteer Chair – for a list of all volunteers
- Underwriters Chair – for a list of those who donated money
- Procurement Chair – for a list of those who donated auction items
- Reservations Chair – for a list of guests
- Cashiers Chair – for a list of winning bidders. If a guest happens to be a winning bidder, thank them for being a winning bidder AND a guest in one thank-you letter.

14.2 Mail questionnaire to patrons

One of the post-event tasks is the preparation of a Post-event Evaluation. Part of that evaluation includes answers to surveys sent to guests that attended your event. The recipients of the survey answer questions on a self-addressed, stamped postcard and then simply drop the postcard in the mail. Since it would be cost effective to include that "survey on a postcard" in the thank-you letters, the responsibility falls on you to make sure those survey postcards go out. See Prepare a Post-event Evaluation (1.20) for more details.

15. Scrapbook Chair

15.1 Compile the scrapbook

Think of what it would mean to next year's Event Chairperson if you presented him or her (or them) with a scrapbook of all records, receipts, lists of people who helped, and post event-evaluations. The new Event Chairperson and all the other chairpersons would not have to reinvent the wheel. They could learn from the mistakes made from the previous year and capitalize on the things that were done right.

Depending on the magnitude of your event, your scrapbook could be as small as a binder full of material, or as large as a half dozen boxes full of records and material. The information in the scrapbook will be very valuable. Don't you think it will be easier to secure the next Event Chairperson if they know a scrapbook is available from which to get information from the last event? It would be frightening for them to think they are starting with nothing. Having a compiled scrapbook will be very helpful when trying the get someone to accept the responsibility of becoming the next Event Chairperson.

The scrapbook can contain spreadsheets, receipts, notes, records and photos. Consider putting the following in your scrapbook

- Event Fact Sheet (1.12)
- Post-Event Evaluation (1.20)
- Names and contact information of chairpersons, volunteers, donors, vendors, entertainers, guests, celebrities, caterer and Auctioneer
- Meeting notes
- Donor-slip sample (4.2)
- Silent Auction Bid Sheet sample (11.4)
- Live Auction Bid Sheet sample (12.11)

- Remember the Date Postcard sample (7.2)
- Invitation sample (7.6)
- Press Kit sample (5.1)
- Newsletter sample (5.3)
- Advertising samples (5.7)
- Any other form sample
- Certificate of Appreciation sample (12.23)
- Printed Program sample (9.1)
- Photographs (15.2)
- Videos (15.3)

15.2 Photograph all event activities

Take photographs to record the planning meetings and planning parties, all the way through the end of the event, including centerpieces and displays and clean-up. Include these pictures in the scrapbook. Try to get a picture of every volunteer doing their volunteer thing. Take pictures of the entertainment and the silent and live auctions. These pictures will be used in the newsletter. Also take pictures of patrons at the party and send them the photo. Put pictures in a PowerPoint presentation to show at the post auction party.

If someone purchased an entire table (7.5), take a picture of everyone seated at that table. Then send copies of the picture to the person who purchased the table. On each purchased table will be a sign with the table purchaser's name on it to help you send the right picture to the right table purchaser. Make sure you get that name in the picture.

If a Table Host (7.6) has filled a table with friends, take a picture. Send copies to the table host to distribute to his or her friends that attended.

Take pictures that you can use as a sales tool for next year's event. Take pictures that show the number of guests that attended your event. Take pictures of banners, signage, and other methods that were used to recognize the generosity of donors. These pictures will be used to get in-kind services, underwriting and auction item donations next year.

15.3   Videotape portions of the event

Consider video taping the event. The video tape can be shown during the post-event party and will be an important part of the Scrapbook (15.1). You don't have to record the event from beginning to end. Video some of the guests arriving and being greeted, video the silent auction, the centerpieces, a portion of the entertainment, part of the live auction, etc. Try to video tape all of your volunteers doing their volunteering. They'll be looking for themselves when you show the video.

15.4   Keep accurate records

Remind all chairpersons to keep accurate records for the Post-Event Evaluation (1.20) and the Thank-you letters that will go out (14.1). It might be a good idea to provide a Post-Evaluation Form to the chairpersons at the beginning of the event planning process, so they will know what they will be expected to report on.

Three-Week Countdown

I often meet with event organizers two or three weeks before their event to make sure certain things get done. At that meeting I ask that certain tasks be completed that will help achieve **The Four Objectives of a Successful Fundraiser.** I have found when those objectives are met, it's easier for me, as the Auctioneer, to conduct a successful live auction. If I were to sit down with you and your committee, here is the agenda I would follow:

The Printed Program

Depending on how elaborate your printed program is, a good portion of it might already be done by now, and not subject to change. It's been my experience, however, that many organizations can still make modifications even this close to the event. So I address it here.

The person designing your printed program will, no doubt, create the layout under good light, while wearing reading glasses, being completely sober, and having intimate knowledge of each live auction item. Fancy fonts and flowery descriptions might seem tempting. When in reality, the people who read your program will do so under dim light, having left their reading glasses at home, after having had a few drinks, and without any previous knowledge about the live auction items. Remember, you must write the program for your guests, not you.

I suggest you make the printed program as easy to read as possible, and make the item descriptions attention-grabbing. The following recommendations pertain to the description of the live auction items in the printed program.

Make it easy to read. Use a large font size: 12 or 14 points is good. Use an easy-to-read font. I suggest Times New Roman, which is the font newspapers use because it is easiest to read in print form.

Number each live auction item. The numbers should correspond to the order in which the live auction items will be on display and auctioned off.

Use descriptive headings. Each item should have a heading and each heading should describe what the item or package is. For example, use "Spa and Massage" rather than "Ladies night out". Imagine if the headings in this book were not descriptive, forcing you to read all the paragraphs to understand the headings. I think you would get discouraged. If your guests are forced to read entire descriptions to understand what each item is about, they may get tired of reading. Also, the headings should be bold in order to stand out.

Use bullet items to highlight the features. Guests like to see at a glance what the features of the item are. They do not want to have to read the entire description to determine what the item or package is about.

After the bullet items, then expound on the details. You can make the rest of the description just as detailed and creative as you like.

Include the retail value. Guests like knowing what the auction item is worth. Don't inflate the value thinking you might get more. People don't mind bidding above retail value when they've been treated right and feel good about spending money with you.

Include the donors. Donors usually want to see their names in print in your program. This recognition is a small price to pay for their generous donations. I like to set their names off in italics to make them stand out a little. After all, without your donors, you wouldn't have items or services to sell.

Write the bid number on the back of the program. If you are not using bid paddles or bid cards to display bid numbers, the back of the program works pretty well. The color of the back of the program should be white to make the bid numbers easy for the Auctioneer to read from a distance. See To Use Bid Numbers or Not (1.9) for considerations regarding whether or not to use bid numbers.

Make the bid numbers big. The Auctioneer needs to be able to see all the bid numbers from the stage. You can use a wide permanent marker to write the bid numbers. Make the bid number tall and wide. If your fist can cover the bid number, then the bid number is too small.

The printed program is explained in detail along with examples under the task called Design the Printed Program (9.1).

Displaying Live Auction Items

Display all live auction items in one place. Do not scatter the items around the area. Put them in a convenient place where guests can easily look them over during social hour.

Display a large sign that says "Live Auction". There should be no mistaking the live auction items from the silent auction items. The sign will also draw guests over for a peek at the live auction items.

Number each item. Make the number big enough to be easily seen without having to bend over and squint. Then display them in the same order as they are in the printed program.

Display something for each item. Packaging has a lot to do with how much attention a product gets. If you can display the actual item, that's the best. Otherwise, display something that represents it. For example, display a Hawaiian lei, some seashells and a big poster for a trip to Hawaii. Display tees and golf balls for 18 rounds of golf. Don't display a gift certificate. Rather, display something that will catch people's attention.

Display a description of the item. It can be the same description as contained in the printed program. Make it big enough for guests to read without having to bend over.

Move the live auction items to the stage area. This should be done before the live auction begins so the items can be shown during the live auction.

More details can be found under the task called Display of Live Auction Items (12.3).

The Live Auction

I like to put show-business into the live auction. The more entertaining, interesting, and fun the live auction is, the better your chances that your guests will get caught up in the thrill of bidding. When guests get caught up in the thrill of bidding, they tend to be more generous, and stick around longer. The suggestions here are meant to bring a little show-biz into your live auction.

Make sure the sound system is a good one (10.25). I cannot emphasize this enough. You are doomed if you use a poor sound system. The extra money spent on a good sound system will be well worth it. You'll need two microphones; one for the Auctioneer and one for the Item Describer (discussed below). A wireless microphone will allow the Auctioneer to roam around the stage and into the audience, making the auction more entertaining.

Make an emotional appeal (1.18). This should take place just before the live auction begins. An emotional appeal can be a short video, PowerPoint presentation, or speech about why it's so important to raise money. You want to get everyone's eyes just a little misty before you launch into the live auction.

Use an Item Describer (12.14). I like to work with a person who describes the items. He or she describes the item and I auction it off. Guests see two different faces, hear two different voices; it makes the auction more interesting. It also gives the Auctioneer a needed rest between items, and allows the Item Describer some time to prepare to announce the next item.

Use an Item Displayer (12.13). An Item Displayer is someone who displays the items or whatever is displayed in place of the items.

Use Bid Spotters (12.16). Bid Spotters are people scattered among the audience and are the eyes of the Auctioneer. They help the Auctioneer recognize bids by pointing and yelling "YUP!" when someone bids. Good Bid Spotters can also be entertaining. If Bid Spotters do their job, you will make more money. Not because they try to convince people to bid, but the mere pointing and yelling tends to give bidders a moment of attention and that feels good to them. When bidders feel good, they are likely to bid again. Don't underestimate the importance of good Bid Spotters. As a rule of thumb, use one Bid Spotter for every 50 guests.

For Auctioneers Only

The information presented in this book is for Auctioneers as much as it is for organizers. As the Auctioneer, you become a resource for organizations. They rely on you to make their live auction successful and trust that you will use all of your accumulated experience, knowledge and skill to get the highest bids possible from your audience. The guidelines and strategies in this book will help you do that.

Throughout this book I have referred to **The Four Objectives of a Successful Fundraiser**. You should make yourself familiar with them for two reasons: First, you are in a good position to become a consultant to organizations putting on fundraising auctions. That will make you more valuable. Second, if the organizers have done a good job achieving the first three objectives, your job will be easier.

Let me give you a possible scenario of what could happen if neither you nor the event organizers paid any attention to **The Four Objectives of a Successful Fundraiser**.

Let's say it is the night of the fundraiser. No attention has been paid to making the guests feel important. They feel ignored. By auction time they have become bored or uninterested. Nothing has been done to instill in guests a desire to support the organization's cause. The guests feel indifferent about helping to support it. No marketing of the live auction items have taken place. In fact, the first time your audience sees the items is when you present them during the live auction.

You are up on stage, alone, in front of everyone, trying to motivate a bored, indifferent, clueless audience to bid high.

You may be a very good Auctioneer, but if the audience does not feel pampered, has little desire to support your cause, and hasn't had a chance to drool over the live auction items, the chance of having a successful auction is pretty slim. And when the auction is not as successful as the organizers had hoped, who do you suppose gets the blame? You do. The Auctioneer is the perfect scapegoat. I know because in the beginning of my auction career, it happened to me. Here are some ideas that have helped me. Now I pass them on to you.

Visit and observe other fundraisers. Observe how well **The Four Objectives of a Successful Fundraiser** are realized. Watch the Auctioneer conduct the live auction. Notice what affect he or she has on the audience. Is the audience having fun with the Auctioneer or are they busy talking among themselves, or even worse, looking bored and disinterested.

Practice your bid calling. Get so good you don't have to think about it. Practice, practice, practice. Visit lots of auctions – fundraising, auto, household, business liquidations, consignment, and livestock auctions. Pay attention to the Auctioneer. You will learn some things to incorporate into your auction style, and probably some things to avoid doing as well. Watch how they encourage people to bid and how they praise people after they bid. Write down the comments they use to make the audience laugh and feel good.

Videotape yourself conducting an auction. As painful as it might be to watch yourself, you will probably pick up on little things you can change to become better.

248

Become an advisor. Meet with the fundraising committee and review **The Four Objectives of a Successful Fundraiser**. If they don't know about these four objectives, and you teach them, you will be looked on as an authority. Your advice will enable them to raise more money than they would have raised otherwise, and you will most likely be invited back next year.

Call the Auction Chairperson a couple of days before the fundraiser just to confirm that you haven't forgotten. Chairpersons are such worriers. Calling them will give them one less thing to worry about. They'll appreciate that.

Dig up some interesting information to add to some of the auction items. If I can get my hands on the live auction item list a couple days in advance, I'll get on the internet and find some interesting bits of information to enhance the description of some of the auction items like vacation spots or restaurants. "Did you know that this restaurant won the 'Best Steak in Town Award' in so-and-so magazine? Their carrot cake is to die for." I think that impresses the organizers and perhaps generates another bid or two.

Here is something I did that was fun. I was selling a private suite of tickets to a baseball game that included a barbeque dinner. I told the audience, "I did some arithmetic and determined this would make a good investment. If you ask each one of your attending guests to donate $25 to this fine organization by paying you back, not only will you recoup the money you spend tonight, but make an extra $100. That's 10% interest in 3 months. You'd be smart to buy this package." The audience laughed. I don't know if my idea generated higher bidding, but it made the bidding fun.

It is little things like this that will set you apart from other Auctioneers who simply show up and call the auction.

Arrive at the fundraiser early. Knowing you are there, and knowing you are an expert, will bring a sense or relief to stressed-out chairpersons.

Check the microphones. Make sure the microphones to be used during the live auction are working well. Always do a sound check and make friends with the sound technicians.

Meet with the volunteers. Arrange to meet with your Bid Spotters (12.16), your Item Describer (12.14), your Item Displayer (12.13), your Item Number Displayer (12.12), your Clerk (12.18) and your Runners (12.17) before the live auction begins. Make sure everyone understands what they are supposed to be doing. Don't assume they have been trained. In many cases, the short meeting you have with them will be their first and only training meeting. Make sure everyone knows what to do. Do some practice yelling with the Bid Spotters and assign them areas to watch during the live auction.

Speak clearly for the Clerk. Make sure the Clerk (12.18) hears the winning amount and the winning bid number so he or she can record them accurately. I like to repeat them: "Sold for five hundred dollars to bidder number 79. Five hundred dollars. 79 the bidder."

Be an entertainer. People go to fundraisers expecting to be entertained and have fun. When you hit the stage, consider yourself to be in show-business. Never use off-color humor, or demeaning comments like, "Come on. I thought we were here to raise money." I heard an Auctioneer once say to someone who was bidding against another person, "If he's going to buy this item, let's make him pay a lot for it." Comments like that might offend someone.

Instead, use positive encouragement. "You're gonna love this trip". Give praise after someone has bid. "I'm with you at $900. I'm glad you came tonight." Or, "I like your

250

style." Stand relaxed and confident. *Your bid-calling should be easy to understand.* Show enthusiasm. Be sincere. Have fun.

Ask the donor to donate another one. Let's say you are selling a private magic show performance by a professional magician. The magician is in the audience. Before the auction starts, approach the magician and ask for a second donation. Introduce yourself and say, "Mr. Magician, I think your private magic show is going to be very popular among the bidders tonight. Could I talk you into providing two performances for the two highest bidders?"

If you get a positive response, which in most cases I believe you will, you have just doubled the amount of money you will get for that auction item. During the live auction, after the Item Describer has given a description of what to expect at the magician's private performance, recognize the magician by asking him to stand up.

Upon selling the performance to the highest bidder, turn to the magician and through your microphone ask, "Mr. Magician (using his real name, of course), would you be willing to donate two performances?" He nods and you say, "He says yes!" The audience breaks into applause and you thank him. Even though you have already been given permission, asking him during the auction serves to give him public recognition for his generosity and that will make him feel more appreciated.

Then turn to the second highest bidder and say, "I have a second one. Would you like it for the same price as I sold the first one?" He nods and you say, "He takes it!" The audience applauds. The magician feels good. The two buyers feel good. The auction committee feels good. And you are looking good.

This strategy works best when the donor sacrifices only his or her time and talent to make the donation happen. Refer to Services that Can be Sold (4.6). This also works well for certain privileges such as golf and ski passes, and tickets to social events like concerts, plays and movies.

I did this at an auction where I auctioned off a famous piano player's private concert. When I asked the next highest bidder if he wanted the second concert, a third bidder raised his hand too. The second highest bidder agreed to buy the second private concert and I apologized to the third bidder for not being able to sell him a concert as there were only two available.

An attentive Bid Spotter saw what happened, raced over to the piano player, and explained that a third bidder wanted to buy his private concert for the same price. The piano player agreed to a third private concert. The Bid Spotter then raced over to me and told me the news.

Before I started selling the next item, I turned to the third bidder and said, "Sir, Mr. Piano Player has just agreed to provide a private concert for you. Are you in?" He raised his hand and nodded. "He's in!" I yelled. I thanked the piano player. The audience applauded and we brought in three times the money, which amounted to quite a bit.

Move around. If you stand behind the podium the entire evening, you are going to put half the audience to sleep. The other half won't be asleep because they will already have left. The audience needs to see you in motion to stay entertained. That's why I suggest using a wireless microphone. It gives you freedom to move around. Go out into the audience occasionally.

Just before you go on stage, make sure your microphone is on, your shirt is tucked in, and your zipper is up.